THE DLM

EARLY CHILDHOOD PROGRAM

Skills and Concepts Guide

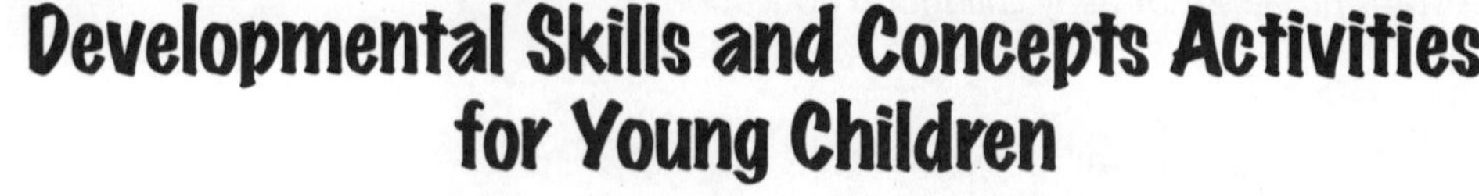

Developmental Skills and Concepts Activities for Young Children

Pam Schiller

Macmillan/McGraw-Hill

Columbus, Ohio

*Pam Schiller, PhD, is an early childhood consultant for SRA Macmillan/McGraw-Hill.
She is a former supervisor and assistant professor of early childhood education.*

ISBN 0-02-685989-0

1 2 3 4 5 6 7 8 9 10 SEC 00 99 98 97 96 95 94

Table Of - CONTENTS

Intellectual Development

Attributes

Sorting and Classifying

Intellectual Development - cont'd

Positioning

Patterning

Motor Development

Gross Motor Movement

Motor Development - cont'd

Motor Development - cont'd

Fine Motor Movement

Introduction

What is The DLM Early Childhood Program Skills and Concepts Guide?

The DLM Early Childhood Program Skills and Concepts Guide presents basic skills and concepts that helps young children develop intellectual and motor skills.The activities presented in the guide cover basic skills and concepts from their lowest level to the level at which most four- and five-year-olds function.

- It may be used alone or in conjunction with any other program.
- It will help you become more aware of the sequential development of thinking and motor skills that help children become independent thinkers and doers. By increasing this awareness, you will be better able to identify strengths and weaknesses and help the children become the best they can be.
- Because of the way the activities in ***The DLM Early Childhood Program Skills and Concepts Guide*** are structured, they not only develop concepts, but they develop vocabulary and language use. These elements provide excellent opportunities for developing language skills in all children, including ESL and bilingual children.

It is not intended that you take a child through this book from beginning to end. Instead, use those activities that each child needs to develop to his or her fullest potential.

Using The DLM Early Childhood Program Skills and Concepts Guide

It is important to keep in mind that

- each child develops and works at his or her own pace
- a child must practice, practice, practice
- at a given time, a child will be strong in some areas of development and weak in others
- the most *normal* can mean is "Here's a general range. *Normal* falls within this range."

As you work with and observe your children, you will notice the areas in which they excel and the areas in which they have difficulty grasping a concept or developing a skill.
This is where ***The DLM Early Childhood Program Skills and Concepts Guide*** will be most helpful.

The DLM Early Childhood Program Skills and Concepts Guide. . .

is divided into two parts: Intellectual Development and Motor Development. In each category, there are activities for developing basic skills and concepts. There is also a hierarchy within each category. Some things come before others—we babble before we talk, we walk before we run, we learn nursery rhymes before we learn Shakespeare.

With these ideas in mind, you may approach this guide in several ways.

- After observing your children for a while, you may decide they're ready to try an activity, let's say classifying. Look at the Table of Contents and choose an activity that seems appropriate for your children. If the activity still seems appropriate after reading it, try it with your children. From that point, move up or down depending on what you observe as you work with the children.

  Continuing with the classifying example, remember that in order to classify objects, a child must have an awareness of physical attributes. It is also helpful for the child to know the language of attributes. If you discover that a child is having difficulty classifying, observe the child carefully and notice the specific areas in which he or she is having trouble. Then ask yourself a few simple questions: Does the child recognize that objects have shape? Can he or she distinguish among shapes? Does the child know the vocabulary for identifying shapes?

  Once you've answered these questions, you will be able to find other activities that will assist the child in learning to classify.

- Perhaps you're working with a topical unit that includes an art activity that requires cutting and pasting. You may know that cutting is very difficult for your children, so you'll have to adapt the activity in the unit. You might ask the children to tear or you might do the cutting yourself. But to prepare them for future activities that require cutting, you'll want to begin to help your children develop the necessary fine motor skills.

  Again, look at the Table of Contents to see what skills are developed before cutting. Find one that seems appropriate for your children and begin there, moving up or down as needed. Over the next few weeks or months, give them plenty of practice at each level and don't move them up until they're ready. Keep in mind that they will not all move at the same pace.

That's all there is to using

The DLM Early Childhood Program Skills and Concepts Guide.

Attributes

Primary
Primarios

Primary Skills & Concepts

Comparison, classification, exploration

Materials

8 to 10 red cubes, 8 to 10 yellow cubes,
8 to 10 blue cubes

Keep In Mind

- Every object has attributes: color, shape, size, texture, taste, odor.
- Identifying attributes is a prerequisite to many higher-level thinking skills including sorting, classifying, and patterning.
- Your children will probably vary widely in their abilities to identify attributes, so feel free to use these activity suggestions as models for many activities related to themes and topics you cover throughout the year.

Vocabulary

blue	azul
red	rojo
yellow	amarillo
cubes	cubos

Getting Ready

- To relate this activity to the theme or topic you are working with, use theme-related objects. The important thing to remember is that the objects should vary in only one attribute: color. All other attributes must be the same.
- For example if you are doing a unit on dinosaurs, you can use small plastic dinosaurs in red, blue, and yellow. You might draw and cut out pictures of dinosaurs and color them red, blue, and yellow.

Attributes 1 - Colors

Primary Activity

- Show three cubes, one of each color. Line up the cubes—red, blue, yellow. Then, starting from the child's left, point to each cube and name the color.

  "This cube is red. This cube is blue. This cube is yellow."
  "Este cubo es rojo. Este cubo es azul. Este cubo es amarillo."
- Repeat the procedure.
- Ask a child to point to the red cube, the blue cube, and the yellow cube. If he/she makes a mistake, point to the cubes and name the colors again.
- When the child can name the colors in the original positions, change positions and ask the child to find the red cube, the blue cube, and the yellow cube.
- Next, point to a cube and ask the child to name the color. If necessary, go back to the first step.

Levels Of Experience

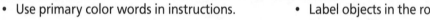

- Use primary color words in instructions.

  "If you are wearing red, you may get in line. All children wearing blue, please stand up."
  "Los que vistan ropa roja que se pongan en fila. Todos los niños que visten azul, párense."
- Ask each child to show what he/she is wearing of that color. Then ask the group whether the color (red) is always the same.

  "¿El color (rojo) siempre es el mismo?"

  They will notice that some (reds) are darker than others. Then have the children line up to show the color from darkest to lightest.
- Label objects in the room.

  "A red chair. A blue book. A yellow box."
  "Una silla roja. Un libro azul. Una caja amarilla."

  Color a square of the appropriate color above each color word.
- Get paint chips or strips that show shades of red, blue, and yellow. If you use paint strips, cut them apart. Have the child arrange each color from darkest to lightest.
- To prepare the children for secondary colors, let them make kaleidoscopes with red, blue, and yellow. You will need water, food coloring, eyedroppers, coffee filters, straight pins or push pins, and pencils. Have the child drop colored water on the coffee filter. He/she will notice that the colors bleed, creating new colors. Put the filter on a pencil eraser with a pin. Have the child twirl the paper.
- *For additional activities with color, see the Levels of Experience activities following Level 10 and the activities for Sorting and Classifying and Patterning.*

Colors Secundarios

Primary Skills & Concepts

Comparison, classification, exploration

Materials

Red, blue, and yellow food coloring, water,
10 to 12 clear plastic glasses on a tray

Vocabulary

blue	azul
red	rojo
yellow	amarillo
green	verde
orange	anaranjado
pink	rosa
purple	morado
food coloring	colorante para comida

Getting Ready

- To relate this activity to the theme or topic you are working with, make a game of it. If for example you are doing a farm unit, pretend that the animals are bored with clear water. During the activity, the children will be making pretty water for the animals to drink.

Attributes 2 - COLORS

Primary Activity

- Fill three glasses with water. Have a child put one drop of red food coloring in one glass, a drop of blue in the second glass, and a drop of yellow in the third glass. Ask the child to name the colors.
- Then have the child pour a little of the red water into an empty glass and then add a little of the yellow water. Ask what happened to the water. If the child does not name the new color, tell him/her that the new color is called orange.
- Follow the same procedure with red and blue to make purple and blue and yellow to make green.
- Point to each of the new colors and name them. Then ask the child to name the new colors. If he/she makes a mistake, point to the colored water and name the colors again.
- When the child can name orange, green, and purple, let him/her combine all three primary colors to see what color he/she can make. Then let the child combine colors from any two or three glasses. Each time name the colors and have the child repeat them.

LEVELS OF EXPERIENCE

- Use color words in instructions.
- Label objects in the room.

  "An orange pot. A purple book. A green truck."

  "Una maceta anaranjada. Un libro morado. Un camión verde."

  Color a square of the appropriate color above each color word.

- Let the children make secondary colors by combining red, blue, and yellow finger paints.
- Let the children make color books. They can cut pictures from magazines and put all of one color on a page. Write the color word, using the appropriate color, on the each page. Bind the pages into a book.

- Go on a color walk. Divide the group into three teams. Assign each team a color. On their walk the children will find objects of each color. When they get back to the room, let each team tell about what they found. Put all of the objects into a learning center for the children to sort.
- *For additional activities with color, see the Levels of Experience activities following Level 10, and the activities for Sorting and Classifying and Patterning.*

Rectangle
Rectángulo

Primary Skills & Concepts

Comparison, classification, exploration

Materials

Cut out outlines of several objects with distinctive shapes, a variety of rectangular cutouts, rectangular parquetry blocks

Vocabulary

rectangular shape forma rectangular

Keep in Mind

- It is important that children understand that shape is an attribute of an object; shape is not an object.
- We do not hand children a shape; we hand them an object with shape. Don't try to explain this to young children; just use the language carefully and mention shape in connection with objects. "Please hand me the cutout shaped like a rectangle. This is a rectangular cutout."
"Por favor pásame el recorte con forma de rectángulo. Esto es un

Getting Ready

- To relate this activity to the theme or topic you are working with, use outlines of theme-related objects.

Attributes 3 - Geometric Shapes

Primary Activity

- Show outlines of several common objects and ask questions about each outline.

  "What is this? How can you tell?"
  "¿Qué es esto? ¿Cómo lo sabes?"

  If the child does not use the word *shape,* tell him/her

  "This is the shape of a (key)."
  "Esta es la forma de una (llave)."

- Give the child several cutouts and ask the children to feel each cutout and tell about its shape.
- Give a child a rectangular parquetry block and ask him/her to tell you about it. Have the child feel the edges of the block. Then ask the child to show you the sides of the block. If necessary, run your hand along the sides, saying

  "This is a side. This is a side. This is a side. This is a side. The shape of the block has four sides."
  "Esto es un lado. Esto es un lado. Esto es un lado. Esto es un lado. La forma del bloque tiene cuatro lados."

  Follow the same procedure with corners.

- Show other parquetry blocks and rectangular cutouts, asking similar questions about several of them. Then ask the child

  "How are all of these rectangular shapes alike?"
  "¿En qué se parecen todas estas formas rectangulares?"

  If necessary, point out that all rectangles have four sides and four corners. (Rectangles have other attributes, however, you probably don't need to mention those at this point.)

- Then give the child a group of cutouts of common objects and rectangles. Have the child sort the cutouts into two groups—those that have a rectangular shape and those that don't.

Levels Of Experience

- Use words that describe shape when giving instructions.
- Have the child locate other objects in the room that have a rectangular shape.

- Label objects in the room.

  "This book has a rectangular shape. This table has a rectangular shape."

  "Este libro tiene forma rectangular. Esta mesa tiene forma rectangular."

- Put a box of objects and cutouts of shapes in a box in the learning center. Have the child sort them into groups and ask him/her to describe the groups.
- *For additional activities with shape, see the Levels of Experience activities following Level 5 and Level 10 and activities for*

Triangle
Triángulo

Primary Skills & Concepts

Comparison, classification, exploration

Materials

Rectangular and triangular parquetry blocks, rectangular and triangular cutouts

Vocabulary

rectangular shape	forma rectangular
triangular shape	forma triangular

Geometric Shapes

Primary Activity

- Show a rectangular and triangular parquetry block of the same color, and ask the child to tell how they are alike and how they are different. Then give him/her another block and ask which block it goes with and why. Continue until the child has two piles of blocks, some rectangular and some triangular.
- Give the child a triangular block and ask him/her to tell you about it. Have the child feel the edges of the block. Then ask the child to show you the sides of the block. If necessary, run your hand along the sides, saying

  "This is a side. This is a side. This is a side. The shape of the block has three sides."

  "Esto es un lado. Esto es un lado. Esto es un lado. La forma de este bloque tiene tres lados."

  Follow the same procedure with the corners.
- Show other parquetry blocks and cutouts, asking

  "How are all of these shapes alike?"

  "¿En qué se parecen todas estas formas?"

  If necessary, point out that all rectangles have four sides and four corners and all triangles have three sides and three corners.
- Give the child a group of cutouts and ask him/her to put the things shaped like a triangle in one pile and those shaped like a rectangle in another pile.

  Turn the rectangles and triangles at a variety of angles and see whether the child can identify them.

Levels Of Experience

- Use words that describe shape when giving instructions.
- Have the child locate other objects in the room that have a triangular shape.

- Label objects in the room.

  "This eraser has a triangular shape. This stool has a triangular shape."

  "Este borrador tiene forma triangular. Este banquillo tiene forma triangular."

- Have the children make their own triangle books. Cut several sheets of drawing paper or construction paper into a triangular shape. Have the children cut pictures of triangular shaped objects from magazines and paste them in their books. Let them dictate descriptive statements about the objects.
- *For additional activities with shape, see the Levels of Experience activities following Level 5 and Level 10 and the activities for Sorting and Classifying and Patterning.*

Circle
Círculo

Primary Skills & Concepts

Comparison, classification, exploration

Materials

Rectangular, triangular, and circular cutouts of the same color, circular cutouts in a variety of sizes

Vocabulary

rectangular shape	forma rectangular
triangular shape	forma triangular
circular shape	forma circular

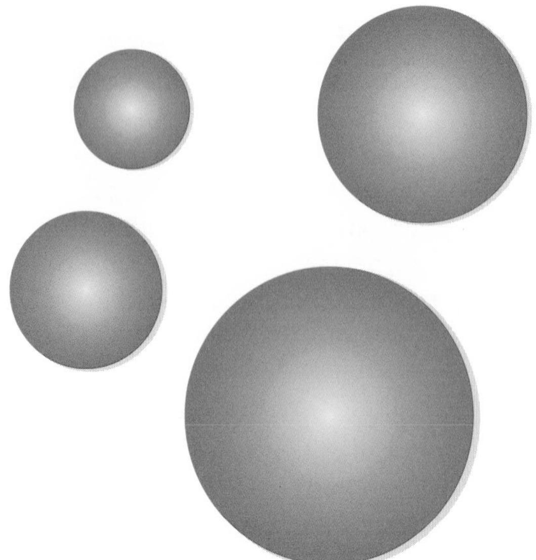

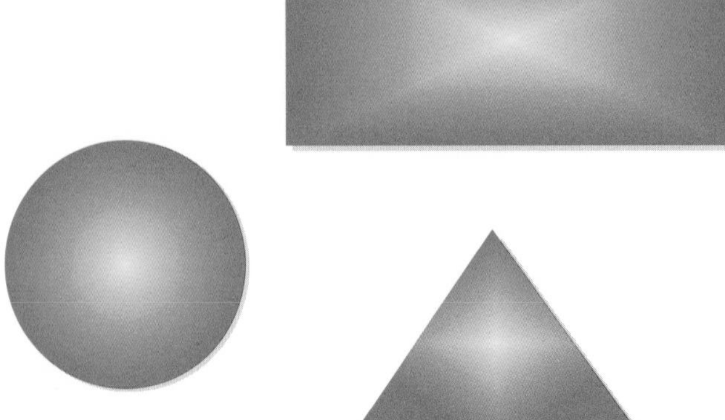

Attributes 5 - GEOMETRIC SHAPES

Primary Activity

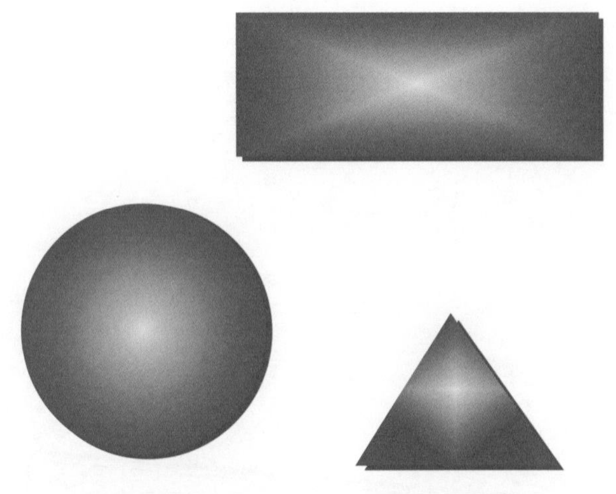

- Give the child a rectangular, triangular, and circular cutout of the same color. Ask the child to tell how they are alike and different.

  "¿En qué se parecen? ¿En qué se diferencian?"

  If necessary, have the child feel the shapes and identify the sides and corners. He/she will discover that one of the cutouts does not have sides and corners.

  "¿Cómo se llaman los recortes que tienen lados y esquinas?"

- Give the child several of each kind of cutout and have the child put all of the cutouts without sides and corners into a pile. Ask the child to name the cutouts with sides and corners.

  Then tell the child that the remaining cutouts are shaped like circles.

  "Los recortes que quedan son círculos."

- Help the child identify objects in the classroom that have a circular shape. Some children will also be able to name objects they cannot see at the moment but are familiar with.

LEVELS OF EXPERIENCE

- Use words that describe shape when giving instructions.
- Have the child locate other objects in the room that have a circular shape.
- Cut sponges into geometric shapes for sponge painting.
- At snack time provide a variety of crackers and dry cereal for the children to sort into piles by shape. Of course, they'll eat them.

- Label objects in the room.

  "The bottom of this glass has a circular shape. This basketball has a circular shape."

  "La parte de abajo de este vaso tiene forma circular. Esta pelota de básketbol tiene formacircular."

- Have the children make rectangular, triangular, and circular shapes with clay and then use those shapes to make designs or objects.

- In the woodworking center, put scraps of wood cut into geometric shapes. Let the children see what they can build with the shapes, nails, and glue.
- *For additional activities with shape, see the Levels of Experience activities following Level 10 and the activities for Sorting and Classifying and Patterning.*

Large, Small, Larger, Smaller
Grande, pequeño, más grande, más pequeño

Primary Skills & Concepts

Comparison, classification, exploration

Materials

Several boxes that look alike except for size; several large and small objects that are similar except for size, such as books, trucks, pencils, stuffed toys

Vocabulary

large	grande
small	pequeño
larger	más grande
smaller	más pequeño
largest	el/la más grande
smallest	el/la más pequeño(a)

KEEP IN MIND

- Most four-year-olds have a basic understanding of large and small or big and little. They learn from experience that large and small are relative. Because they learn this by making hundreds of comparisons, you should use this activity many times with a variety of objects.
- When asked to identify something large, the chances are the child will choose something larger than he/she. The same is true with small. Children tend to compare an object's size to their own size.

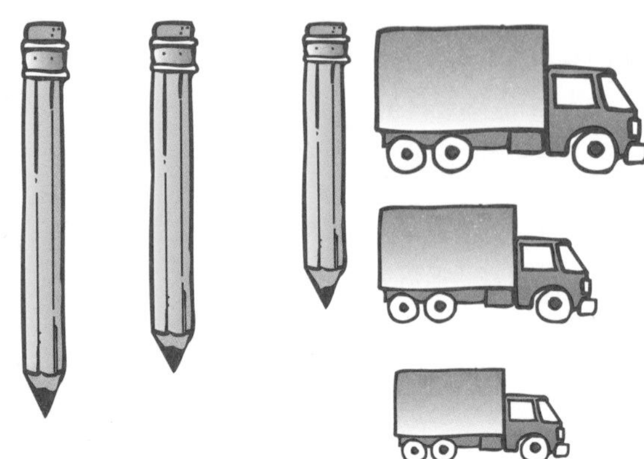

Primary Activity

- Place a large box and a very small box in front of the child so that the large box is at his/her left. Point to each box in turn and say

  "Are these boxes the same size? This is a large box. This is a small box. Which box is large? Which box is small?"
  "¿Son del mismo tamaño estas cajas? Esta caja es grande. Esta caja es pequeña. ¿Cuál es grande y cuál es pequeña?"
- Remove either box and put a new box in its place. Again, point to each box and tell whether it is large or small. After you have done this several times, ask the child to tell without prompting which box is large and which is small.
- Repeat the procedure with other objects that are similiar except for size.
- Then ask the child to find something in the room that is large.

  "Busca algo en el salón que sea grande."

 **LEVELS OF EXPERIENCE** 

- To introduce *larger* and *smaller*, repeat the procedure above saying

  "Are these boxes the same size? This box is larger than this one. This box is smaller than this one. Which box is larger? Which box is smaller?"

  "¿Son estas cajas del mismo tamaño? Esta caja es más grande que la otra. Esta caja es más pequeña que la otra. ¿Cuál de las cajas es más grande? ¿Cuál de las cajas es más pequeña?"

  After you have done this several times, ask the child to find things that are larger than he/she and then things that are smaller.

- To introduce *largest* and *smallest*, repeat the procedure using three boxes arranged in order from largest to smallest and the words *largest* and *smallest*. Rearrange the boxes and repeat.
- Play Larger Than a Wastebasket. Show the wastebasket and ask the child to name something that is larger than the wastebasket, something that is too big to fit in the wastebasket.

  "¿Qué es más grande que el cesto de la basura? ¿Qué cosas son tan grandes que no caben en el cesto de la basura?"

  You can also use this game with teams and with the word *smaller*.

- Give the children several objects that are similar except for size and let them arrange the objects in order from largest to smallest or from smallest to largest.
- When the children are able to arrange similar objects, give them objects that vary greatly in appearance.

Height
Altura

Primary Skills & Concepts

Comparison, classification, exploration

Materials

Tin cans or cylinders of approximately the same diameter but of varying heights

Vocabulary

taller	más alto
shorter	más bajo
tin can	latas
cylinders	cilindros
tallest	el/la más alto(a)
shortest	el/la más bajo(a)

Keep in Mind

- Height refers to one dimension vertically, length to one dimension horizontally.
- When an object is viewed in its vertical position, we refer to its height and to how tall it is in comparison to another object.
- When the object is viewed in a horizontal position, we refer to its length and to how long it is.
- It is important that we begin discussing height with objects that are normally viewed in a vertical position.

Primary Activity

- Ask the child whether he/she is taller than you and how he/she might prove it.

  "¿Eres más alto/a que yo? ¿Cómo lo sabes?"

  If necessary, stand beside the child and show that your head is higher than the child's. Then ask the child what things in the room are taller than you and what things are taller than he/she.

  "¿Qué cosas del salón son más altas que yo? ¿Y más altas que tú?"

- Stand two cylinders or tin cans of different heights on the same level surface. Ask the child which is taller and how he/she knows. If the child has difficulty, point to the appropriate can as you say

  "This can is tall. This can is short. This can is taller than this can. The top of this can sticks up higher than the top of this can."
  "Esta lata es alta. Esta lata es baja. Esta lata es más alta que la otra lata. La tapa de esta lata llega más alto que la tapa de esta otra lata."

  Repeat the procedure with additional pairs of cans or cylinders.

- Give the child two cylinders and let him/her tell which is taller. Repeat this several times.
- Repeat the procedure with *shorter*.

Levels of Experience

- Introduce *tallest* and *shortest* in a similar manner, always using three cylinders. Let the child put the cylinders in order from tallest to shortest and from shortest to tallest.
- Give the children objects that are similar except for size and let them arrange the objects in order from tallest to shortest or from shortest to tallest. Remember the arrangements should go from left to right.
- Tape a long sheet of butcher paper to the wall and mark each child's height and date it. Measure each child several times throughout the year so he/she can see that they are growing.
- When the children are able to seriate similar objects, give them objects that vary greatly in appearance.
- Take a Height Walk. Encourage the children to find things that are taller and shorter than they are.
- During cleanup ask the children to arrange objects in order by height: books, cans of paint, paintbrushes, dolls, potted plants.
- In the block center, the children can see who can build the tallest block tower. Yes, the towers will fall over and be knocked down.

Length
Longitud

Primary Skills & Concepts

Comparison, classification, exploration

Materials

Several strings of different lengths, several objects that can be compared for length, shoes, toy vehicles, tableware

Vocabulary

longer	más largo
shorter	más corto
longest	el/la más largo(a)
shortest	el/la más corto(a)

Keep In Mind

- It is important that we begin discussing length with objects that are normally viewed in a horizontal position.

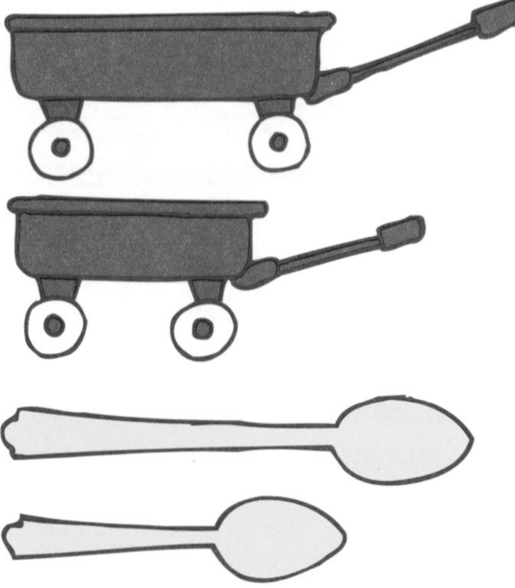

Attributes 8 - SIZE

Primary Activity

- Ask the child whether his/her foot is longer than yours and how he/she might prove it.

  "¿Cuál es más largo, tu pie o el mío? ¿Cómo lo sabes?"

  If necessary, have the child put his/her foot next to yours with your heels aligned.

- Place two strings of different lengths on the table in front of the child. One end of each string should be aligned on the edge of the table. Ask the child which string is longer. If the child has difficulty, point to the appropriate string as you say

  "This string is long. This string is short. This string is longer than this string because this string sticks out farther than this string."
  "Esta cuerda es larga. Esta cuerda es corta. Esta cuerda es más larga que la otra porque llega más lejos."

  Repeat the procedure with other pairs of strings.

- Give the child two strings and let him/her tell which is longer. Repeat this procedure several times. Then give the child other pairs of objects to compare for length.
- Repeat the procedure with *shorter*.

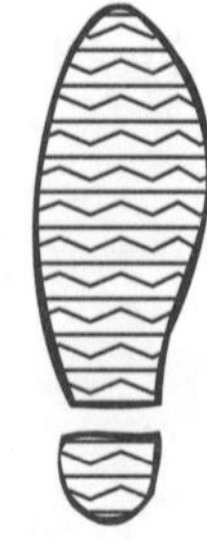

LEVELS OF EXPERIENCE

- Introduce *longest* and *shortest* in a similar manner always using three strings. Let the child put the strings in order from *longest* to *shortest* and from *shortest* to *longest*.
- Give the children several objects that are similar except for size and let them arrange the objects in order from *longest* to *shortest* or from *shortest* to *longest*. Remember the objects should always be aligned at their bases.

- Trace each child's foot on a sheet of paper and write the child's name on his/her footprint. Cut out the footprints and let the children arrange them in order from *longest* to *shortest*.

- Play Longer Than My Foot. Let the children spend a little time identifying things in the room that are longer than their feet. Then choose a leader. The leader will give clues to help the others guess what the object is. The one who figures out the answer is the next leader. If there is any doubt about the comparative length of an object, of course, the child will have to prove that the object is longer than his/her foot.

Flavor
Sabor

Primary Skills & Concepts

Comparison, classification, exploration

Materials

Table salt, sugar, lemon juice, margarine tubs, ice-cream sticks, a variety of foods that are salty, sweet, and sour such as crackers, pretzels, chips, honey, hard candies, frosting, lemons, limes, dill or sour pickles

Keep In Mind

- With four-year-olds you will probably want to limit taste experiences to those that deal with salty, sweet, and sour.
- If you know that a child is allergic to a particular food, do not let the child taste it. If a child does not want to try a food, do not force him/her.

Vocabulary

salty	salado
sweet	dulce
sour	agrio

Attributes 9 - Flavor

Primary Activity

- Talk with the child about his/her favorite foods and why he/she likes them. The child will probably say

  "It tastes good."
  "Está rico/a."

  Use the words *sweet* and *salty*, but they might not know the word *sour*. Then let the child taste a very small amount of the salt. Talk about salt and how we use it, and help the child name some foods that taste salty.
- Follow a similar procedure with the sugar and lemon juice.
- Let the child sample the foods you have. With each food, encourage the child to talk about the taste and why he/she likes or doesn't like it.

  "Which is saltiest? Which is sweetest? Which is the most sour?"
  "¿Cuál es la más salada? ¿Cuál es la más dulce? ¿Cuál es la más agria?"

Levels Of Experience

- Each time you have a snack or a meal with the children, talk about the foods they are eating and how the foods taste. Model the use of words that describe flavors and textures. Encourage them to identify as many flavors as they can.

- When you are preparing food with the children, talk about the ingredients and let the children taste them. Encourage them to predict whether the final product will be sweet, salty, or sour.

- Use baby-food jars or small margarine tubs with lids to make tasting jars. Paint or cover the containers if necessary so the children cannot see what is inside them. Cut a hole in the top of each lid that is large enough for an ice-cream stick to pass through. Put a different flavor in each jar. The child will dip a stick into the jar, taste the food or flavor, and try to figure out what it is. You might use peanut butter, jelly, applesauce, fruit juice, salt water, and pickle juice.

Texture
Textura

Primary Skills & Concepts

Comparison, classification, exploration

Materials

Oaktag, rough sandpaper, and several materials that are smooth or rough such as silk and burlap, flat wallpaper and embossed wallpaper, finished wood and tree bark, smooth and wrinkled aluminum foil

Vocabulary

smooth	suave
rough	áspero

KEEP IN MIND

- We are going to limit these experiences to objects that can be described as smooth (or slick) and rough. You may, of course, extend the concept to other textures.

Primary Activity

- Give the child a sheet of oaktag and a piece of rough sandpaper. Let the child explore them and then encourage him/her to tell you everything he/she can about the items. If the child does not use words that describe the textures, say something like

  "This sheet of paper is smooth. You can't see or feel any bumps. Do you like the way it feels? Why? This sheet of sandpaper is rough. It's bumpy and it hurts my hand just a little when I rub it. Do you like the way it feels? Why?"
  "Esta hoja de papel es suave. No se ven ni se sienten rugosidades. ¿Te gusta cómo se siente al tocarla? ¿Por qué? Esta hoja de papel de lija es áspera. Tiene rugosidades y me hace daño cuando froto mi mano sobre ella. ¿Te gusta cómo se siente al tocarla? ¿Por qué?"
- One at a time, give the child the other materials to explore and describe. If necessary, talk about the materials as you did with the oaktag and sandpaper.
- Give the child a few minutes to explore the room and to point out things that are smooth and things that are rough. You might want to let the child compare two or three things to find out which is smoother or smoothest and which is rougher or roughest.

LEVELS OF EXPERIENCE

- Make texture big books for the children to explore in a learning center.
- Talk with the children about the textures of the clothes they're wearing.
- Talk about the textures of foods during snack time.
- On a science walk, explore the textures of leaves, grass, dirt, and other objects.
- Have texture days. Ask each child to find something in the room or bring something from home that is rough, smooth, bumpy, or scratchy.

Odor
Olor

Primary Skills & Concepts

Comparison, classification, exploration

Materials

Blindfold (optional); several foods with strong and distinctive odors, such as peppermint, peanut butter, orange, potato chips; several objects with strong and distinctive odors, such as clay, new shoes, nail polish, soap, rubbing alcohol or perfume on a cotton ball, paint

Keep In Mind

- We don't usually label odors in the same way we do flavors. If you ask a child "What does this smell like?" "¿A qué huele esto?" the child will probably tell you that it smells good or bad. Perhaps he/she will name the thing: "It smells like peanut butter." "Huele a mantequilla de cacahuate."
- For this reason, we suggest that you use familiar items with strong and distinctive odors.

Primary Activity

- Talk with the child about things he/she likes to smell and why he/she likes the odors.
- Ask the child to close his/her eyes or blindfold the child. Then let the child smell one of the foods and tell you about it. Continue with several more foods or items.
- After the child has smelled three or four items, talk about which he/she likes best and why.

LEVELS OF EXPERIENCE

- Each time you have a snack or a meal with the children, talk about the foods they are eating and how the foods smell and taste. Model the use of words that describe flavors and odors.
- When you are preparing food with the children, talk about the ingredients and let the children smell them.
- Use baby-food jars or small margarine tubs with lids to make smelling jars. Paint or cover the containers if necessary so the children cannot see what is inside them. Punch a few small holes in the top of each lid. Put a different food or item in each jar. The child will smell each jar and try to figure out what it is. You might use peanut butter, pickles, cinnamon, and cooking extracts such as peppermint, vanilla, almond, and orange.

- Whenever possible, talk about the attributes of an object.

  "Do you like working with clay? What color is the clay? What other things are that color? What does it feel like? Can you think of anything else that feels like clay?"

  "¿Te gusta jugar con plastilina? ¿De qué color es la plastilina? ¿Qué otras cosas tienen ese color? ¿Cómo se siente cuando la tocas? ¿Qué otras cosas se sienten igual al tocarlas?
- Set up an exploration center and change the objects often. Let the children explore freely, but make sure you take the time to talk with them about what they are discovering.

- Let the children make individual books or a class big book about attributes. For example, in a book about large and small, they can paste or draw pictures of objects and label them *large*, *small*, *larger*, *smaller*, *largest*, *smallest*.
- Put magnifying glasses in each of your centers, not just the science center. Everything looks so different when magnified that the children will be encouraged to spend more time and energy exploring and describing.

General
General

Primary Skills & Concepts

Physical attributes, visual discrimination, comparative measurement, left/right discrimination

Materials

Several pairs of shoes of different styles such as a child's tennis shoes, a girl's black dress shoes, a woman's high heels, cowboy boots, a man's loafers, baby booties, ballet slippers, galoshes, thongs

Keep In Mind

- The ability to sort and classify is necessary for almost every activity in which the children participate.
- This ability begins to develop very early; babies sort and classify information when they differentiate between their parents. It is not a skill used in isolation.
- While children are developing the ability to sort and classify, they are discovering, reinforcing, and extending many other abilities. For example, in the first two activities, the children will match pairs of shoes. In doing so, they will be aware of color, shape, length, and left/right, even though they might not be able to name those attributes.
- We begin with this activity because most children are able to match a pair of shoes. While the children are successfully matching, you have the perfect opportunity to help them become aware of the thinking processes they use when sorting and classifying.
- Children should practice sorting and classifying literally hundreds of times at this age, so feel free to use these activity suggestions as models for many activities related to the themes and topics you cover throughout the year.

Matching Pairs

Primary Activity

- Put 3 to 4 pairs of shoes on the floor in a pile. Have a child match pairs of shoes and tell why he/she matched them as he/she did. Encourage the child to tell as much as possible about the shoes.
- To help the child match or to help him/her become aware of the thinking processes involved in matching, you might want to have the child tell which shoes are the same color, which are the same length, which of two shoes is longer, which of a pair is the right shoe and which is the left, or which shoes are tall and which are short. Some children will be able to name the colors of the shoes.

Levels Of Experience

- You will want to do this activity several times with some children. To vary the difficulty, change the number of pairs the children deal with.
- After you have worked with the children on this matching activity, put a box of shoes in a learning center so the children can match the shoes independently.
- *For additional sorting and classifying activities, see Levels of Experience following Level 4 on page 33.*

Alike in One Attribute
Un atributo en común

Primary Skills & Concepts

Physical attributes, visual discrimination, comparative measurement, left/right discrimination

Materials

Several pairs of shoes that are alike in one attribute, such as length or color, and different in others

KEEP IN MIND

- The difference between Level 2 and Level 1 is that the shoes used in Level 2 have a common attribute. If all of the shoes are the same size or the same color, matching becomes a little more difficult.

Primary Activity

- As in the Level 1 activity, put 3 to 4 pairs of shoes on the floor in a pile. Have a child match pairs of shoes and tell why he/she matched them as he/she did. Encourage the child to tell as much as possible about the shoes.
- To help the child match or to help him/her become aware of the thinking processes involved in matching, you might want to have the child tell you in what ways the shoes are alike and in what ways they are different.

Levels Of Experience

- You will want to do this activity several times with some children. To vary the difficulty, increase the number of common attributes. For example, use shoes that are the same size and red or white tennis shoes with different kinds of fasteners.
- After you have worked with the children on this matching activity, put a box of shoes in a learning center so the children can match the shoes independently.
- In the homemaking center, provide other pairs (mittens, gloves, socks) for the children to sort as they "do the laundry."
- Let the children make pairs books. Give them magazines and catalogs so they can tear out or cut out pictures of pairs: shoelaces, earrings, curtains, body parts, twins. Have them paste each pair on a different page. As you talk to the children about their books, you can write the name of the pair on each page.
- Give the children pegboards and colored pegs or golf tees and let them make pairs.
- Let the children make handprints or footprints with washable tempera on construction paper. Cut the prints apart to create a handprint pair puzzle for each child. Put each puzzle in an envelope with the child's name on it. Put the puzzles in the manipulative center.
- *For additional sorting and classifying activities, see Levels of Experience following Level 4 on Card 15.*

By One Attribute, Color
Un atributo, color

Primary Skills & Concepts

Physical attributes, visual discrimination, comparison, exploration

Materials

8 to 10 red cubes, 8 to 10 yellow cubes

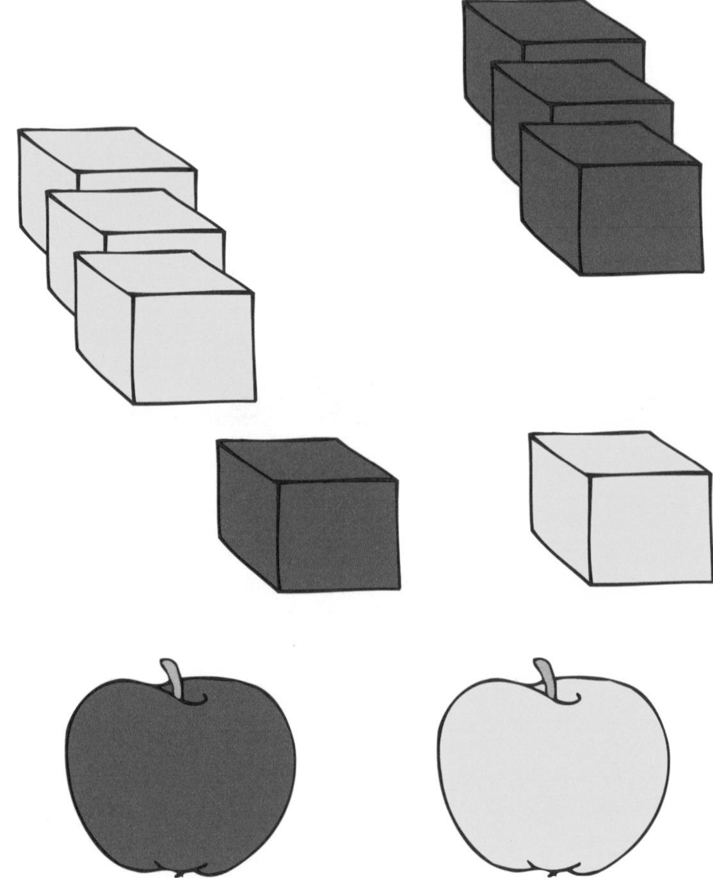

Keep in Mind

- Although most young children can identify and name red, blue, and yellow, they can do this activity without knowing the color names. Use color names as you work with the children and they will soon be familiar with the names.
- You may adjust this activity to fit any topic by using objects that are alike except for color. For example, you may use red trucks and yellow trucks in a transportation unit or red apples and yellow apples in a nutrition unit.

Primary Activity

- Show 1 red and 1 yellow cube. Ask the child to tell how the cubes are alike and different.

  "¿En qué se parecen los cubos? ¿Y en qué se diferencian?"

  Then show more cubes of each color. Point to a red cube and ask the child to make a pile of

  "all of the cubes like this one" or "all of the red cubes."
  "Haz un montón con todos los cubos como éste; o con todos los cubos rojos."

  Ask the child what he/she knows about the cubes that are left over. Point to a yellow cube and ask the child to make a pile of

  "all of the cubes like this one" or "all of the yellow cubes."
  "¿Cómo son los cubos que quedan?"
  "Haz un montón con todos los cubos como éste; o con todos los cubos amarillos."

- Put all of the cubes into a pile and ask the child to make two sets of cubes—a set of red cubes and a set of yellow cubes.

LEVELS OF EXPERIENCE

- After the child is able to sort two colors of cubes, add a third color. As the child progresses, he/she will be able to sort several colors at once.
- After you have worked with the child on this activity, put a basket of color cubes in the learning center for the child to sort independently.
- *For additional sorting and classifying activities, see Levels of Experience following Level 4 on page 33.*

By Color + Another Attribute
Color + otro atributo

Primary Skills & Concepts

Physical attributes, visual discrimination, comparison, exploration

Materials

4 or 5 each, red cubes, red beads, red crayons; 4 or 5 each, yellow cubes, yellow beads, yellow crayons

KEEP IN MIND

- This activity is more difficult than the Level 3 activity because the child is asked to sort by color while being distracted by other attributes.
- You may adapt this activity to fit any topic by using other objects. For example, in a fall unit you might use red leaves, red apples, and red berries and yellow leaves, yellow apples, and yellow berries.

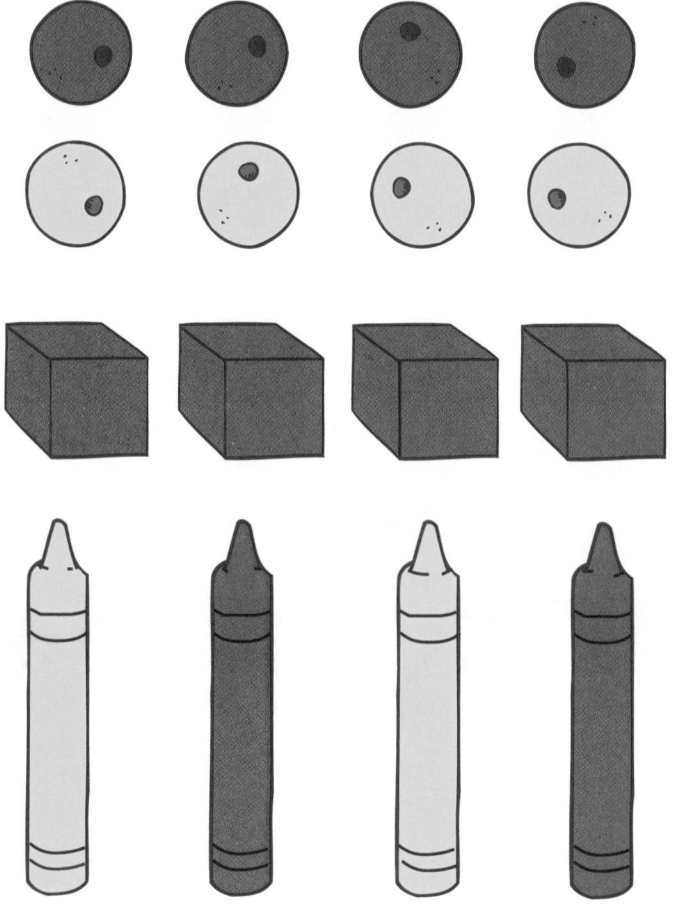

Primary Activity

- Put all of the objects in a pile and ask the child to tell you what he/she knows about them. Then ask the child to find "all of the red things" "todas las cosas rojas" and put them together. Ask the child to tell you how the other things are alike. Have him/her find "all of the yellow things" "todas las cosas amarillas" and put them together.
- Don't be surprised if a child mentions that the objects can be grouped in other ways. Praise him/her for being such a good thinker.

LEVELS OF EXPERIENCE

- Add other red or yellow objects to the group, varying size and shape. Add another set of objects in a third color.
- Put the objects in a learning center and let the child sort them independently.
- Use transition times to reinforce critical thinking skills, such as classifying.

  "If you are wearing red shoes, hop to the door and get in a line. If you have blue eyes, tiptoe to the rug and sit quietly. If you like to eat something that is yellow, walk backward to the art table."

  "Los que tengan zapatos rojos, den saltos hasta la puerta y se ponen en fila. Quien tenga ojos azules, que vaya de puntillas a la alfombra y se siente sin hacer ruido. Quien quiera comer una cosa de color amarillo, que camine hacia atrás hasta la mesa de arte."

- Make a sorting center. You'll need at least three small plastic baskets: one to hold the objects or pictures that will be sorted, and at least two smaller baskets to hold the sorted objects. Tie the baskets together with plastic ties. Label the *smaller* baskets with pictures showing categories for sorting. For example, you might tape a red square to one basket and a yellow square to the other. The child will take the objects out of the large basket and put them into the appropriate small basket. You can add and remove baskets as necessary.

- Take a collecting walk. Before the walk, choose two colors and tell the children that they will be looking for objects of those colors. Talk about what they might find. Give each child an envelope or paper bag to hold the collectibles. When you get back to the room, let the children share their treasures and talk about them. Ask each child to choose two or three things to put in the collection center. Then use all of the collected objects in sorting activities.

By One Attribute, Shape
Un atributo, forma

Primary Skills & Concepts

Physical attributes, visual discrimination, comparison, exploration

Materials

8 to 10 circular shapes cut from colored oaktag or flannel,
8 to 10 triangular shapes cut from colored oaktag or flannel

KEEP IN MIND

- Remember, at this level the child should concentrate on shape, so we want to eliminate the color and size distracters. You may do this activity on a flannel board or on a table.

Getting Ready

- Cut all of the shapes from the same color oaktag or flannel and make them the same size, approximately 2 inches.

Primary Activity

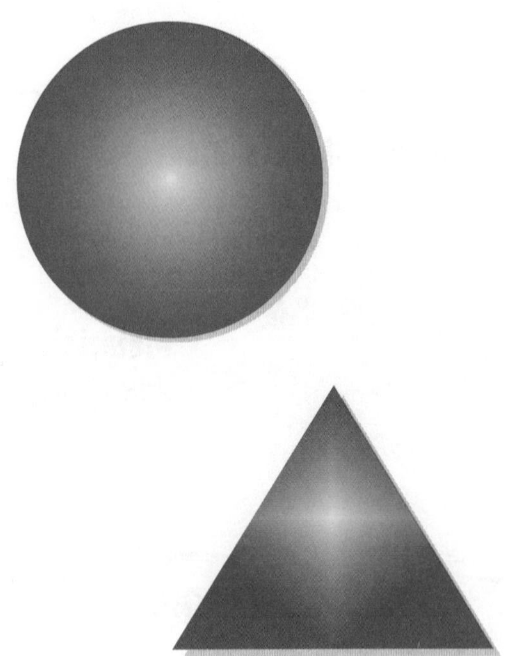

- Give the child a circular shape to examine. Encourage the child to trace around the edge with his/her fingers, with his/her eyes open and then closed. Ask the child to tell about the shape. Some children will use the terms circle or round as they are describing. Then give the child several more circular shapes and ask how they are alike.
- Use the same procedure with the triangular shapes. Then ask the child how the round (circular) pieces and the triangular pieces are alike and different.

  "¿En qué se parecen las piezas redondas (circulares) a las piezas triangulares? ¿En qué se diferencian?"
- Then randomly display the two sets of shapes on the table or flannel board. Point to a circular shape and ask the child to make

  "a set of round shapes" or make "a set of all the pieces just like this one."
  "Haz un grupo con las formas redondas; o con todas las piezas como ésta."
- Point to a triangular shape and ask the child to make

  "a set of triangular shapes" or make "a set of all the pieces just like this one."
  "Haz un grupo con las formas triangulares; o con todas las piezas como ésta."
- Put all of the pieces into a pile and ask the child to make two sets of pieces—a set of round (circular) pieces and a set of triangular pieces.

LEVELS OF EXPERIENCE

- After the child is able to sort two shapes, add a third. As the child progresses, he/she will be able to sort several shapes at once.
- After you have worked with the child on this activity, put a box of plane shapes in a learning center for the child to sort independently.
- *For additional sorting and classifying activities, see Levels of Experience following Level 6 on page 37.*

By Shape + One Attribute
Forma + otro atributo

Primary Skills & Concepts

Physical attributes, visual discrimination, comparison, exploration

Materials

8 to 10 circular shapes cut from three colors of oaktag or flannel,
8 to 10 triangular shapes cut from three colors of oaktag or flannel

Keep In Mind

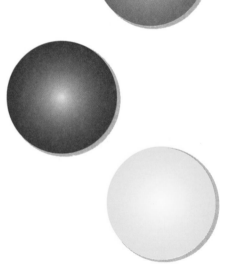

- This level is more difficult than Level 5 because the child is being asked to sort by shape while being distracted by another attribute.

Vocabulary

circular shape	formas circulares
triangular shape	formas triangulares

Getting Ready

- Cut the shapes from the three colors of oaktag or flannel but make them all the same size, approximately 2 inches.

Primary Activity

- Put all of the shapes in a pile and ask the child to tell you what he/she knows about them. Then ask the child to find "all of the round (circular) pieces" and put them together.

  "Busca todas las piezas redondas (circulares) y ponlas juntas."

  Ask the child to tell you how the other pieces are alike. Have him/her find "all of the triangular pieces" and put them together.

  "Busca todas las piezas triangulares y ponlas juntas."

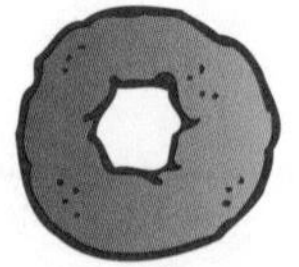

Round Food	Square Food
cereal	soda crackers
banana chips	wheat crackers
soup crackers	graham crackers

LEVELS OF EXPERIENCE

- Add a third shape to the set of pieces.
- Using only two shapes, vary the color and size of the pieces.

- Put the pieces in a learning center and let the child sort them independently.

- Let the children prepare a snack mix with square cereal, round cereal, small soup crackers, banana chips, and small square crackers. Make a chart similar to the one above, labeling the columns with the shapes of the snacks. Display each ingredient in a shallow bowl or plate. Talk about the shape of each. Then ask the children to name the foods that have a round shape. Write the food names in the "round" column of the chart. Do the same with the square shapes. Then ask a child to put a handful of a round food into a large mixing bowl. Ask another child to put a handful of a square food into the mixing bowl. Continue until each child has added an ingredient. Mix and serve.

By Type or Function
Tipo o función

Primary Skills & Concepts

Physical attributes, visual discrimination, comparison, exploration, naming a set, problem solving

Materials

A group of objects, some of which are related, such as a ball, a toy truck, a roller skate, a building block, a doll, a crayon, a pencil, a sheet of paper, a spoon, a fork, a plate, a napkin, a drinking glass

KEEP IN MIND

- If you give children a box of things, they automatically begin to sort them. It's as though they need to organize their world. Of course, we want them to do this and to become good at it because it is a skill they will use in every aspect of their lives. It's the way they relate new information to what they already know.
- At the simplest levels, children group things that are exactly alike, similar, the same color, and the same shape. Then they begin to sort by type and function.

Sorting & Classifying 7 - Classifying

Primary Activity

- Place the objects on the table or floor and describe a set for the child to find. For example, you might say

  "I am thinking of things that have wheels. Make a set of things that have wheels. I am thinking of things that are toys. Make a set of things that are toys."
  "Estoy pensando en cosas con ruedas. Haz un grupo con cosas que tienen ruedas. Estoy pensando en cosas que son juguetes. Haz un grupo con cosas que son juguetes."

- Then put a pile of objects on the floor or table and ask the child to put them into groups. If the child forms a group, ask him/her to tell you about it, to name the group, and tell how the things are alike and different.
- If the child does not form a group, offer help by saying things such as

  "Make a group of things you like to play with. Make a group of things that you can draw with. Make a group of things that are made of paper."
  "Haz un grupo con las cosas con que te gusta jugar. Haz un grupo con las cosas con que puedes dibujar. Haz un grupo con las cosas hechas de papel."

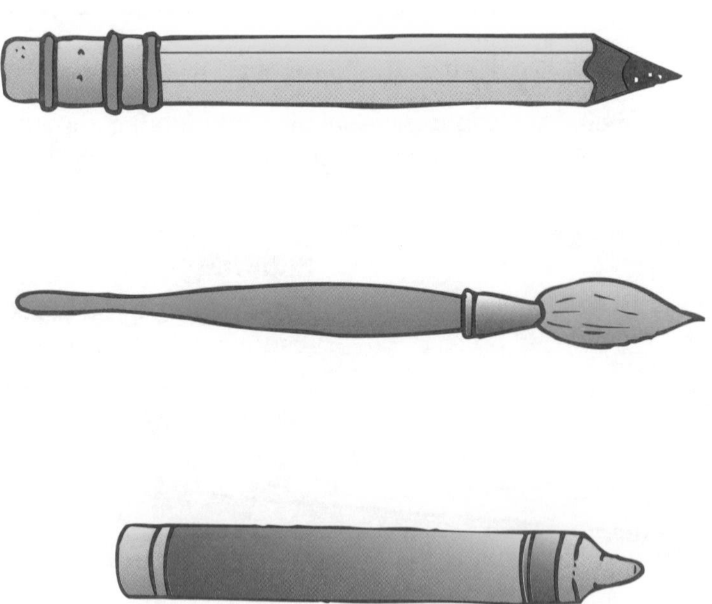

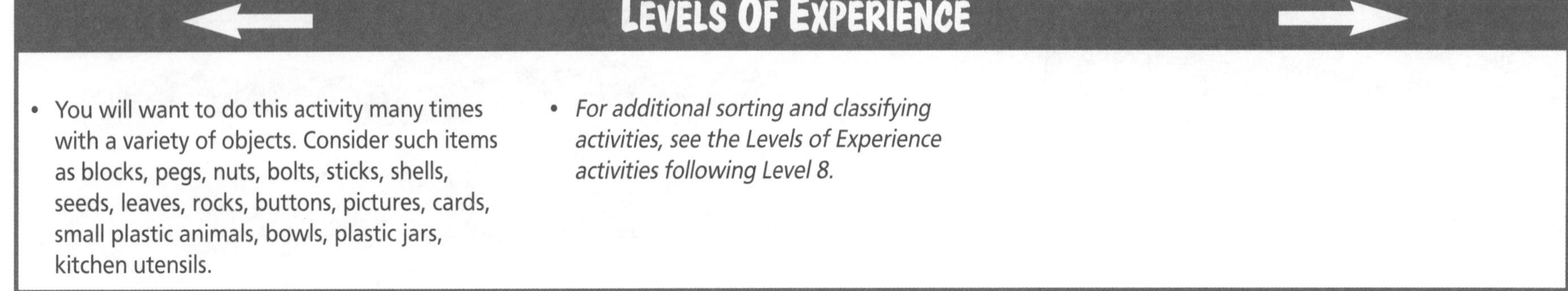

Levels Of Experience

- You will want to do this activity many times with a variety of objects. Consider such items as blocks, pegs, nuts, bolts, sticks, shells, seeds, leaves, rocks, buttons, pictures, cards, small plastic animals, bowls, plastic jars, kitchen utensils.
- *For additional sorting and classifying activities, see the Levels of Experience activities following Level 8.*

What Doesn't Belong?
¿Qué cosa no pertenece a este grupo?

Primary Skills & Concepts

Physical attributes, visual discrimination, comparison, exploration, naming a set, problem solving

Materials

A red crayon, a red block, a red sheet of paper, a yellow balloon
A spoon, a fork, a knife, a toy truck
A pencil, a ruler, a stick, a ball
Additional groups of objects that are related in some way such as by color, shape, or function

KEEP IN MIND

- One way to tell whether children have a good grasp of sorting and classifying is to ask "What doesn't belong?" "¿Qué cosa no pertenece a este grupo?" This is a complicated thinking procedure that requires the child to analyze the attributes or functions of the items, think of several categories into which the items might fall, and finally, decide on one category that will exclude an item.

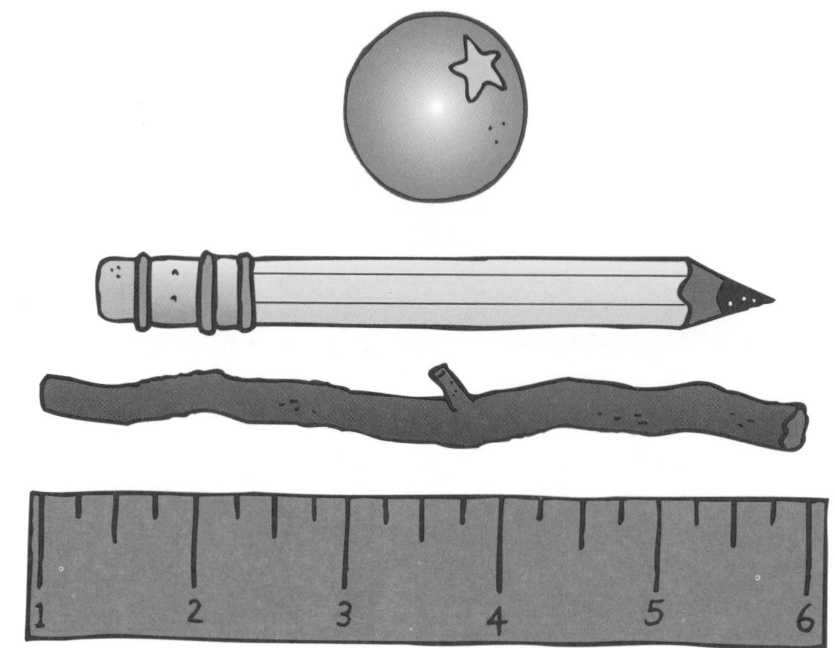

Primary Activity

- Show the red crayon, red block, red paper, and yellow balloon and ask

  "What doesn't belong? Why?"
  "¿Qué cosa no pertenece a este grupo? ¿Por qué?"

- If the child has difficulty, compare two red items, asking

  "How are they alike? How are they different?"
  "¿En qué se parecen? ¿En qué se diferencian?"

  Add a third red item, asking

  "Is this one the same color? Does it belong?"
  "¿Es éste del mismo color? ¿Pertenece a este grupo?"

  Add the yellow balloon, asking

  "Is this one the same color? Does it belong? These three things are red. This is yellow.
  The yellow one does not belong."
  "¿Es éste del mismo color? ¿Pertenece a este grupo? Estas tres cosas son rojas. Esta es amarilla. La amarilla no pertenece a este grupo."

- Continue in the same way with other groups of objects.

LEVELS OF EXPERIENCE

- As often as possible use classifying in conversation.

  "Please bring me all of the blue blocks. Put away all of the paintbrushes. Put all of the crayons in the red basket. Put all of the glue bottles on the blue tray. I see that you put the cans of food on the top shelf. Where did you put the boxes of food?"

  "Por favor, tráeme todos los bloques azules. Guarda todos los pinceles. Pon todos los crayones en el cesto rojo. Pon todos los botes de pegamento en la charola azul. Ya vi que pusiste las latas de comida en el estante más alto. ¿Dónde pusiste las cajas de comida?"

- Use the "not" sign with your sorting center. For example, put an assortment of toy cars in the collection basket. On one small basket, tie a picture of a car inside a black circle. On the other basket, tie a picture of a car inside a black circle with a diagonal line through it. The child will sort into two groups: thosethings that are toy cars and those that are not toy cars.

- Could there be a more logical way to encourage sorting and classifying than a class grocery store! All it takes is a few bags, a basket or two, a toy cash register, shelves, and empty food containers. Most parents will happily recycle clean, safe food containers for the class store.

By Multiple Attributes
Varios atributos

Primary Skills & Concepts

Physical attributes, visual discrimination, comparison, exploration, naming a set, problem solving

Materials

Theme-related shapes, oaktag, markers

KEEP IN MIND

- It is very difficult for most four-year-olds to keep two attributes in mind when they're sorting and classifying, so don't expect it. It won't hurt, however, for you to expose more advanced children to this type of thinking. Begin with concrete activities and do them in two stages.

Getting Ready

- You might use a theme-related shape, such as a teddy bear. Make several copies of the shape on oaktag and cut them out. Divide the bears into two sets and color all of the members of each set the same way. For example, make one set of brown bears with red bows and one set of white bears with green bows.

Primary Activity

- In stage one, you will show the child all of the objects and ask him/her to "make a set of bears."
  "Haz un grupo con osos."

  If the child has any difficulty, don't go to stage two. Go back and review Levels 1–8 of Sorting and Classifying.
- Now, stage two. Ask the child to "make a set of bears that are brown and have red bows."
  "Haz un grupo con osos que sean de color café y lleven un lazo rojo."

  If the child has difficulty, ask him/her "What are you going to do?"
  "¿Qué vas a hacer?"

  Then repeat while demonstrating. Have the child "make a set of bears that are white and have green bows."
  "Haz un grupo con los osos que sean blancos y que lleven un lazo verde."

LEVELS OF EXPERIENCE

- Do not expect perfection. You will need to do this activity many times and in many contexts. Change the objects periodically.

- When you are giving instructions or talking with the children, use the *and* statement.

  "Will you bring me something that will hold crayons and has a top? What does a bird eat that is red and grows on trees? I like your picture of flowers that are tall and yellow."

  "¿Qué cosa sirve para poner los creyones y tiene tapa? ¿Qué comen los pájaros que es rojo y crece en los árboles? Me gusta tu dibujo de las flores altas y amarillas"

- *For additional classifying activities, see the Levels of Experience activities at the end of on page 45.*

By Multiple Attributes
Varios atributos

Primary Skills & Concepts

Physical attributes, visual discrimination, comparison, exploration, naming a set, problem solving

Materials

Theme-related shapes, oaktag, markers

Vocabulary

some	algunos
all	todos

KEEP IN MIND

- This procedure is similar to the procedure in the Level 9 activity. The only real difference is the words *some* and *all*. Young children often have difficulty understanding that some is less than all.

Getting Ready

- Again, you might use a theme-related shape, such as a teddy bear. Make several copies of the shape on oaktag and cut them out. Divide the bears into two sets and color all of the members of each set the same way.

Primary Activity

- Show all of the bears and say to the child

  "Here are some shapes. How are they alike? How are they different? All of these are shaped like bears. Some of the bears are brown. Give me some of the bears. Give me the brown bears."
  "¿En qué se parecen las formas que hay aquí? ¿En qué se diferencian? Todas tienen forma de oso. Algunos son de color café. Pásame algunos osos. Pásame los osos de color café."

  If necessary, repeat and demonstrate.

- Do this several times, each time changing the attribute: the white bears, the bears with red bows, the bears with green bows.

- If the child is not having difficulty, say to the child

  "Give me all of the bears."
  "Pásame todos los osos."

  Then place the bears randomly on the table. Now combine the some and all statements with the and statement.

  "I am going to ask you to give me some of the bears. Give me all of the bears that are brown and have red bows."
  "Voy a pedirte que me des algunos de los osos. Pásame todos los osos de color café y que tengan un lazo rojo."

  If necessary, repeat and demonstrate.

LEVELS OF EXPERIENCE

- When you are giving instructions or talking with the children, use the *and* statement.

  "All of the children who are wearing jeans and T-shirts may get in line. Here are all of the trucks. Some do not have wheels. Give me all of the trucks that do not have wheels."

  "Todos los niños que llevan camiseta y pantalones vaqueros que se pongan en fila. Aquí están todos los camiones. Algunos no tienen ruedas. Pásame todos los camiones que no tienen ruedas."

- Design your sorting center so the children can sort using the *and* statement. Label the box with two symbols. For example, place a set of clown shapes in the collection box. Label the two sorting boxes with pictures that show red hats and frowns and blue hats and smiles.

- Here are a few more combinations to sort: red buttons with two holes/blue buttons with four holes; white socks with blue stripes/blue socks with white stripes; and brown cookies with white frosting/white cookies with brown frosting.

Top & Bottom
Arriba y abajo

Primary Skills & Concepts

Following directions, spatial and directional awareness, vocabulary development, comparison

Keep In Mind

- A position word tells where a thing is in relation to something else.
- Position words can be adverbs or prepositions, can have more than one meaning and use, and many can be used interchangeably. To add to the confusion, usage varies from one region of the country to another, and most regions use some redundant prepositions.
- You might want to adjust these activities to reflect the usage in your region.
- *Top* is used to mean the highest part when the object is in the upright position. *Bottom* is used to mean the lowest part when the object is in the upright position.
- Use the activities that follow as models for many activities related to the themes and topics you cover throughout the year.

Materials

Objects with obvious tops and bottoms such as boxes with lids, a plate, pieces of furniture, index cards, tape

Vocabulary

top	arriba
bottom	abajo

Getting Ready

- Make two sets of cards. On each card write the word *top* or *bottom, arriba* or *abajo.*

Positioning 1 - Top & Bottom

Primary Activity

- Show an object with an obvious top and bottom such as a box with a lid. Put your hand on the lid, and tell the child

  "My hand is touching the top of this box."
  "Mi mano está tocando la parte de arriba de esta caja."

  Put your hand on the bottom of the box and say

  "Now my hand is on the bottom of the box. The top is high. The bottom is low. The top is higher than the bottom."
  "Ahora, mi mano está en la parte de abajo de la caja. La parte de arriba es alta. La parte de abajo es baja. La parte de arriba está más alta que la parte de abajo."

  Let the child identify the top and the bottom of the box.
- Repeat the procedure with several other objects.
- Point out objects in the room and ask the child to

  "Touch the top of the (bookcase). Touch the bottom of the (pencil sharpener)."
  "Toca la parte de arriba de la (estantería). Toca la parte de abajo del (sacapuntas)."
- Show a word card that says *top/arriba*. Tell the child what the word is and ask him/her to

  "Tape the card to the top of (the table)."
  "Pega la tarjeta en la parte de arriba de la (mesa)."

  Have the child tape *top/arriba* cards to the top of several other objects. Follow the same procedure with *bottom/abajo* cards.

top/arriba

Levels Of Experience

- Give the child a stack of objects such as socks, napkins, spoons, papers, or books. Ask the child to give you the (sock) that is on the top of the stack and then the (sock) that is on the bottom of the stack. Continue until the stack is gone.
- Use snack time to reinforce top and bottom. Give one child a stack of plastic glasses and a tray. Ask the child to put each of the glasses on the tray with the top up. Give another child a stack of napkins and ask him/her to spread the napkins on top of the table. Ask a third child to put a graham cracker on top of each napkin.
- *See the Levels of Experience activities following the Level 6 activity for activities that deal with several position words.*

Over & Under
Encima de y debajo de

Primary Skills & Concepts

Following directions, spatial and directional awareness, vocabulary development, comparison

Materials

Table, doll or stuffed toy, ruler or yardstick

Vocabulary

over	encima de
under	debajo de

Keep in Mind

- The words *over* and *under* are interchangeable with *above* and *below*. We are using *over* and *under* because children usually use those words first. You may, however, use either pair. *Over* is used to mean *above* and not touching a surface and across and down. *Under* is used to mean beneath and not touching a surface and down and across.

Over & Under

Primary Activity

- Display a table and a doll or stuffed toy. Hold the doll over the table and say

  "I am holding the doll over the table. Where is the doll?"
  "Pongo la muñeca encima de la mesa. ¿Dónde está la muñeca?"

  Follow a similar procedure while holding the doll under the table. Then ask the child to position the doll over and under the table.
- Repeat the procedure holding the doll over and under the ruler. Have the child hold the doll over and under a variety of his/her body parts such as the head, arm, leg, and foot.
- Give the child several two-step directions that require him/her to place the doll over and under objects in the room.

  "Go to the wastebasket. Hold the doll over the wastebasket." "Go to the reading center. Hold the doll under the chair.''
  "Acércate al cesto de la basura. Pon la muñeca encima del cesto. Acércate a la mesa de lectura. Pon la muñeca debajo de la silla."

Levels Of Experience

- As you look through a picture book with the child, find objects in the *over* and *under* positions and ask the child to locate them.

- Hold a rope or yardstick at different heights and ask the child to go *over* and *under* it.
- Set up an obstacle course using objects the child can go *over* and *under*. On each object tape a card with the word *over* or *under* printed on it.

- *See Levels of Experience following the Level 6 activity for experiences dealing with several position words.*

On & Off

Primary Skills & Concepts

Following directions, spatial and directional awareness, vocabulary development, comparison

Materials

Table, doll or stuffed toy, several small toys

Vocabulary

on
off

Keep In Mind

- The word *on* is used to mean above and in contact with a surface or object. The word *off* is used to mean away from a surface or object.
- *On* and *off* are relative positions; when we say that an object is "off the table," we are at least implying that it was at one time "on the table." The children will be less confused if you always begin with *on*.

Positioning 3 - On & Off

Primary Activity

- Display a table and a doll or stuffed toy. Put the doll on the table and say "The doll is on the table. Where is the doll?" Take the doll off the table and say "The doll is off the table. Where is the doll?" Then ask the child to position the doll on and off the table.
- Repeat the procedure holding the doll on your lap and off your lap. Have the child hold the doll on and off a variety of his/her body parts and surfaces in the classroom.

Levels Of Experience

- Use the words *on* and *off* whenever possible as you describe and give instructions.

  "Jason, please take the books off the table and put them on the top shelf of the bookcase."

- Play Simon Says with *on* and *off*.

- Let the children make "On and Off" books. Give them old magazines and let them cut out pictures that show objects or people in on and off positions. After the children have pasted the pictures in their books, talk to them about the pictures and write phrases that describe the picture. "The chair is on the floor." "The hat is off the man's head."
- *See the Levels of Experience activities following the Level 6 activity for activities that deal with several position words.*

In & Out
Dentro y fuera

Primary Skills & Concepts

Following directions, spatial and directional awareness, vocabulary development, comparison

Materials

A box or basket, several small classroom objects

in/dentro

Vocabulary

in	dentro
out	fuera

out/fuera

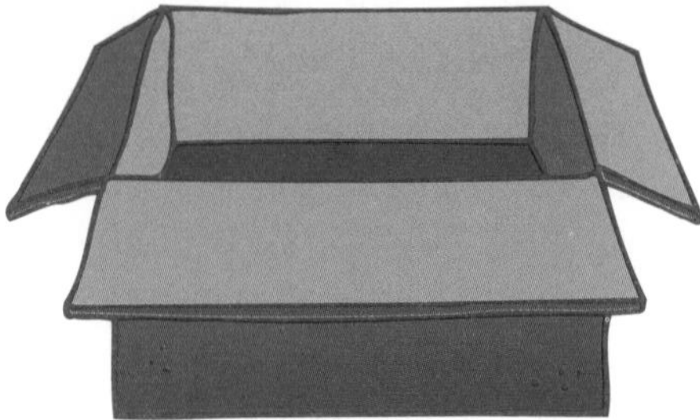

Keep In Mind

- The words *in* and *out* are often interchangeable with *into*, *inside*, and *outside*.
- We are using *in* and *out* because children usually use those words first. You may, however, use the words most common in your region.
- *In* is used to mean contained or enclosed. *Out* is used to mean away from the enclosure or container.

Primary Activity

- Display a box and a small object such as a toy truck. As you put the truck in the box, say

  "I am putting the truck in the box. The truck is in the box. Where is the truck?"
  "Estoy poniendo el camión dentro de la caja. El camión está en la caja. ¿Dónde está el camión?"

  Take the truck out of the box and say

  "I am taking the truck out of the box. What did I do with the truck?''
  "Estoy sacando el camión fuera de la caja. ¿Qué he hecho con el camión?"

- Ask the child to put the truck in the box and take it out. Encourage him/her to describe the actions.

  "Pon el camión dentro de la caja y luego sácalo fuera de la caja."

- Continue having the child place objects in the box and take them out, each time describing the action.

Levels Of Experience

Give directions for other activities that require in and out actions.

"Go out the door. Come into the room. Put the blocks in the toy chest. Take all of the crayons out of the box. Get the red paper out of the closet.''

"Sal fuera del salón. Vuelve a entrar al salón. Pon los bloques dentro del cajón. Saca los creyones fuera de la caja. Saca el papel rojo fuera del armario."

- Play In and Out the Window. Have the children form a circle and hold hands. The child who is "It" stands in the center. As the group sings, the children in the circle raise their joined hands and the child who is "It" threads his/her way around the circle by going under the raised hands. The words to the song are "In and out the window. In and out the window. In and out the window as I have done before.''

  "Dentro y fuera de la ventana. Entro y salgo por la ventana."

- *See the Levels of Experience activities following the Level 6 activity for activities that deal with several position words.*

Front & Back
Delante y atrás

Primary Skills & Concepts

Following directions, spatial and directional awareness, vocabulary development, comparison

Materials

Objects with clearly distinguishable fronts and backs such as a clock, a book, a dollhouse; objects without clearly distinguishable fronts and backs such as an apple, an orange, a ball

Vocabulary

front	delante
back	atrás

KEEP IN MIND

- *Front* is used to mean the part that faces forward. We often think of the front as being the most important. *Back* means the part that faces backward.

Primary Activity

- Have the child point to the front and then to the back of his/her head. Talk about how the front and back of the head are different. Then ask the child questions that will help him/her draw conclusions about front and back.

  "Do you watch the front or the back of a television? Do you start at the front or the back of a book? Do you look at the front or the back of a picture?"

  "¿Qué miras, delante o atrás del televisor? ¿Por dónde empiezas a mirar los libros, por delante o por atrás? Cuando miras una fotografía, ¿la miras por delante o por atrás?"

- Display an object with a distinctive front and back such as a clock. Point to the front of the clock and say

  "This is the front of the clock."

  "Esta es la parte de delante del reloj."

  Point to the back and say

  "This is the back of the clock."

  "Esta es la parte de atrás del reloj."

  Ask the child to point to the front and back of the clock.

- Show other objects with distinctive fronts and backs. Ask the child to identify the front and back and tell how he/she knows.
- Add to the group of objects items that do not have distinctive fronts and backs. Ask the child to choose an object and identify the front and back and tell how he/she knows. Continue until the children recognize that some objects do not have a front and back.

LEVELS OF EXPERIENCE

- Extend the idea of *front* and *back* to include in front of and in back of by having the child hold objects in front of and in back of himself/herself.
- Display a line of toy cars. Point to a car and ask

  "What is in front of this car? What is in back of this car?"

  "¿Qué hay delante de este carro? ¿Qué hay atrás de este carro?"

  Continue pointing out several cars.

- Give the child a set of toy cars. Place one on the table and say to the child

  "Put a red truck in front of this blue truck. Put a green truck in back of this blue truck."

  "Pon un camión rojo delante del camión azul. Pon un camión verde atrás del camión azul."

  Continue having the child add cars to the line in this manner.

- Do similar activities using colored blocks or stringing beads.

- *See the Levels of Experience activities following the Level 6 activity for activities that deal with several position words.*

First, Next, & Last
Primero, siguiente y último

Primary Skills & Concepts

Following directions, spatial and directional awareness, vocabulary development, comparison

Materials

Colored inch cubes or toy trucks or cars

Vocabulary

first	primero
next	siguiente
last	último

FIRST, NEXT, & LAST

Primary Activity

- Have four children form a line by giving directions such as these.

  "(Maria), stand here. (Jason), stand in back of (Maria). (John), stand in back of (Jason). (Debbie), stand in front of (Maria).
  "(María) párate aquí. (Jason) ponte atrás de (María). (John) ponte atrás de (Jason). (Debbie) ponte delante de (María)."

  Point to each child and describe his/her position using the words *first*, *next*, and *last*, *primero, siguiente y último*. Then ask the other children to tell who is first, next, and last in line.
- Move the children so they are in different positions and repeat the activity.
- Give the children colored cubes or toy vehicles. Have the children make rows of the cubes or toys following your instructions. Use the words *first*, *next*, and *last* in your instructions. When the children have made a row, ask questions about the objects and encourage the children to answer using the words *first*, *next*, *last*, *in front of*, and *in back of*, *primero, siguiente, último, delate y atrás*

LEVELS OF EXPERIENCE

- Play Simon Says using any of the position words presented in this section.
- Use position words in one- and two-step directions for manipulatives.

  "Put a block on the table. Put a block on the table and a truck under the table."

  "Pon un bloque sobre la mesa. Pon un bloque sobre la mesa y un bloque debajo de la mesa."

- Play Where Is Willie. Position Willie, a child or a stuffed toy. To the tune of "Paw-Paw Patch" sing "Where, Oh, Where is Our Little Willie?" In the last line of the song tell where Willie is.
  "Where, oh, where is our little Willie? Where, oh, where is our little Willie? Where, oh, where is our little Willie? Sitting on the chair."
- As a variation of Follow the Leader, give a direction using a position word; for example, "Show us *on*." Each child then finds a way to show *on*. The child might sit on a chair, put a doll on a table, put his/her hands on his/her head. Each child would then tell about what he/she did to show *on*.

- Play What Is It? Rather than describing what an object looks like, describe its position and let the children try to figure out what it is. For example, say "I am thinking of something. It is on top of the piano. It is in front of the drum. What is it?"

Patterning

Two Objects by Color
Dos objetos por color

Primary Skills & Concepts

One-to-one correspondence, visual discrimination, left-to-right progression, sequence

KEEP IN MIND

- A pattern is a model that is repeated.
- Awareness of patterns and the ability to predict patterns are essential to critical thinking because patterns are part of both the physical and mental worlds.
- Children who are not aware of patterns or do not use what they know about patterns must rely on rote memory, so they view their worlds as disconnected pieces of information.
- This activity is limited to patterns of two objects with one variable—color.
- The activities on the next page should be used as models for many activities related to the themes and topics you cover throughout the year.

Materials

Colored inch cubes or red and black checkers

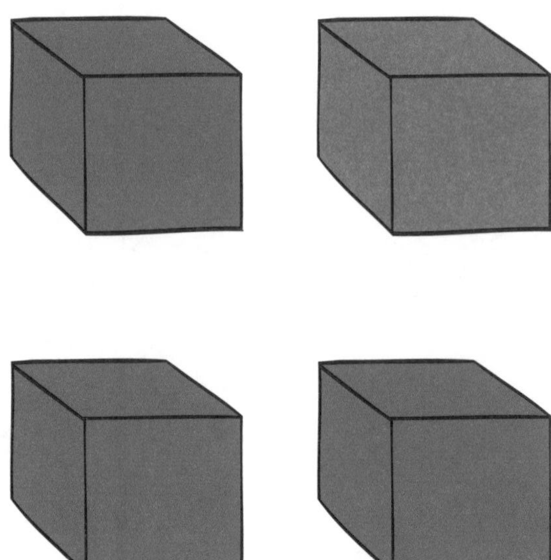

Patterning 1 - Horizontal

Primary Activity

- Choose several cubes or checkers in two colors. (We'll use red and blue cubes.) Tell the child that you are going to make a pattern. From the child's left to right display a red cube, saying

  "My pattern starts on your left. First, I'll use a red cube. Next, I'll use a blue cube. This is my pattern. Red cube. Blue cube."

  "Mi patrón empieza por la izquierda. Primero, pongo un cubo rojo. El siguiente será un cubo azul. Este será mi patrón. Cubo rojo. Cubo azul."
- Make and describe the pattern again directly below the first pattern. Then ask the child to make the pattern. If the child does not describe the pattern as he/she makes it, you describe it. Continue until the child can make and describe the pattern.
- Change colors and repeat the procedure several times. You may use two blocks that are the same color.
- Let the child initiate a pattern for you to reproduce.

Levels Of Experience

- Use other objects or pictures of objects that vary only in color.

- Make pattern cards. Draw colored cube patterns or checkers patterns on index cards. Put them in a learning center with the colored inch cubes or checkers so the child can work independently.
- Make patterns of colored stars for the child to reproduce.

- Cut out and color pictures of theme-related items for the children to use in patterning. Make pattern cards to go with the shapes. For example, in the fall you might make leaves, pumpkins, or apples. You could make dinosaurs, teddy bears, or clown faces.

Repeating Two Objects by Color
Repetir dos objetos por color

Primary Skills & Concepts

One-to-one correspondence, visual discrimination, left-to-right progression, sequence

Materials

Colored inch cubes, red and black checkers, or colored beads and string

Keep in Mind

- Repeating a two-item pattern is a logical extension of the Level 1 activity.

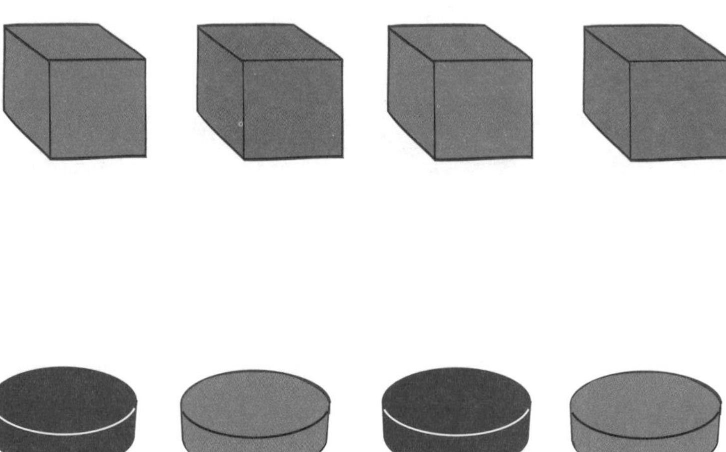

Patterning 2 - Horizontal

Primary Activity

- From the child's left to right display a red cube, saying

  "My pattern starts on your left. First, I'll use a red cube. Next, I'll use a blue cube. This is my pattern. Red cube. Blue cube. Now I'm going make my pattern again."
  "Mi patrón empieza por la izquierda. Primero, pongo el cubo rojo. El siguiente es el cubo azul. Este es mi patrón. Cubo rojo. Cubo azul. Ahora voy a seguir haciendo mi patrón."

- Place a red cube and then a blue cube next to your first pattern so that you have red, blue, red, blue. Describe the pattern and then say

  "What color cube do I put next?"
  "¿De qué color será el siguiente cubo?"

- If the child does not recognize that red comes next, begin at the child's left and touch and name each cube.

  "Red. Blue. (pause) Red. Blue."
  "Rojo. Azul. (Pausa) Rojo. Azul."

  Have the child touch the cubes and name the colors.

- Continue repeating the pattern until the child can make and describe the pattern.
- Change colors and repeat the procedure several times. You may use two blocks that are the same color.
- Let the child initiate a pattern for you to reproduce.

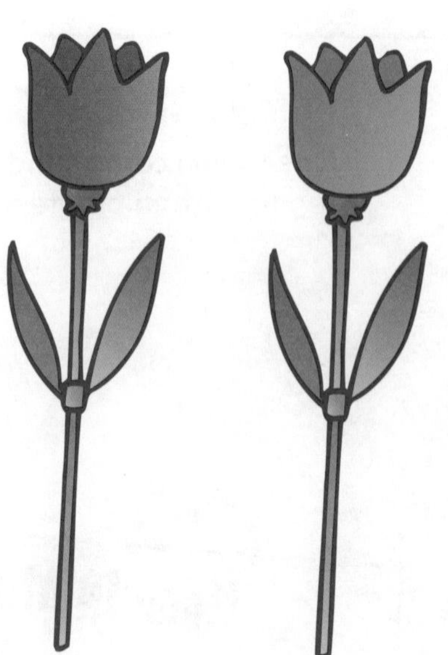

Levels Of Experience

- Use other objects or pictures of objects that vary only in color.
- Let the child string beads in patterns.
- Encourage the child to see how long he/she can make the pattern string.
- Let the child use pattern cards as models for repeating patterns.
- Pair children and let them take turns initiating, copying, and repeating patterns.
- Hang a clothesline at the child's level. Let him/her hang colored paper napkins or socks in repeating patterns.
- Put plastic flowers at the sand table and let the child plant a garden of flowers in repeating patterns.
- Give the child colored shapes of paper to arrange in patterns and paste to another sheet of paper.

Two Objects by Color
Dos objetos por color

Primary Skills & Concepts

One-to-one correspondence, visual discrimination, top-to-bottom progression, sequence

Materials

Colored inch cubes or red and black checkers

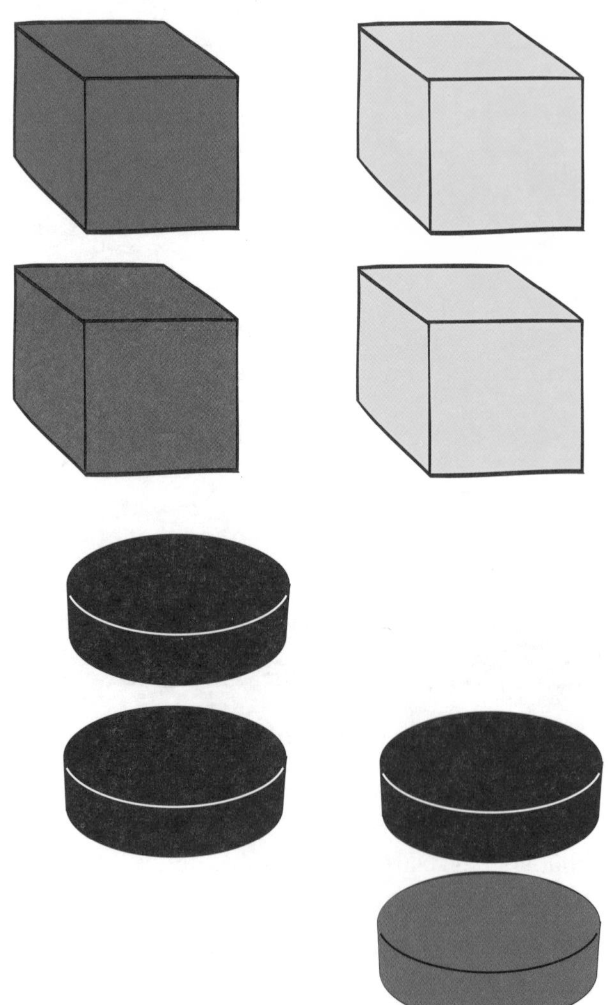

Keep In Mind

- In this activity the child will reproduce vertical patterns limited to patterns of two objects with one variable—color. It is basically the same as the Level 1 activity, but the orientation is changed.

Primary Activity

- Choose several cubes or checkers in two colors. (We'll use red and blue cubes.) Tell the child that you are going to make a pattern. Display a red cube, saying

  "My pattern starts here. First, I'll use a red cube. Next, I'll use a blue cube. I put the blue cube below the red cube. This is my pattern. It goes from top to bottom. Red cube. Blue cube."

  "Mi patrón empieza aquí. Primero pongo un cubo rojo. El siguiente será un cubo azul. Pongo el cubo azul debajo del cubo rojo. Este es mi patrón. Va de arriba a abajo. Cubo rojo. Cubo azul."
- Make and describe the pattern again directly beside the first pattern. Then ask the child to make the pattern. If the child does not describe the pattern as he/she makes it, you describe it. Continue until the child can make and describe the pattern.
- Change colors and repeat the procedure several times. You may use two blocks that are the same color.
- Let the child initiate a pattern for you to reproduce.

LEVELS OF EXPERIENCE

- Use other objects or pictures of objects that vary only in color.

- Make pattern cards. Draw colored cube patterns or checkers patterns on index cards. Put them in a learning center with the colored inch cubes or checkers so the child can work independently.

- Make patterns of colored stars for the child to reproduce.
- Cut out and color pictures of theme-related items for the children to use in patterning. Make pattern cards to go with the shapes. For example, in the spring you might make leaves, flowers, or birds. You could make farm animals, trucks, or children's faces.

Repeating Two Objects by Color
Repetir dos objetos por color

Primary Skills & Concepts

One-to-one correspondence, visual discrimination, top-to-bottom progression, sequence

Materials

Colored inch cubes, red and black checkers, or colored beads and string

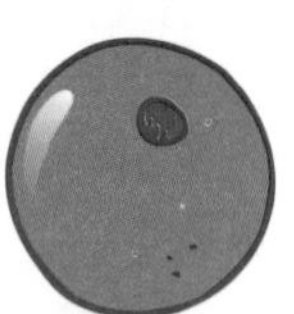

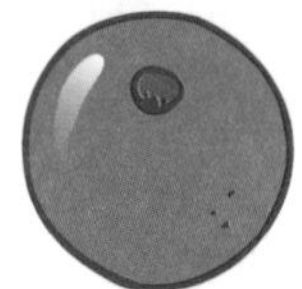

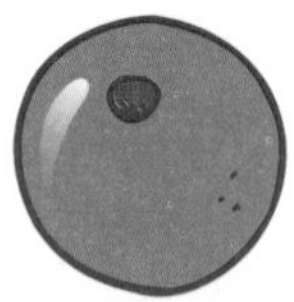

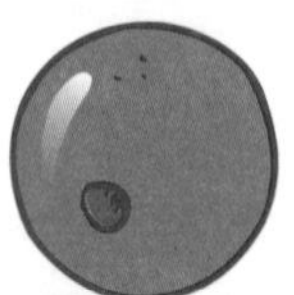

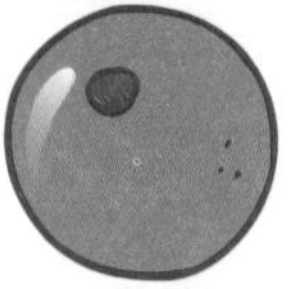

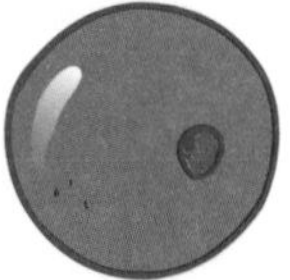

Keep In Mind

- This is basically the same as the Level 2 activity, but the orientation is changed.

Primary Activity

- Display a red cube, saying

  "My pattern starts here. First, I'll use a red cube. Next, I'll use a blue cube. I put the blue cube below the red cube. This is my pattern. Red cube. Blue cube. Now I'm going to make my pattern again."
  "Mi patrón comienza aquí. Primero, pongo el cubo rojo. El siguiente será el cubo azul. Pongo el cubo azul debajo del cubo rojo. Este es mi patrón. Cubo rojo. Cubo azul. Ahora vuelvo a hacer mi patrón."

  Place a red cube and then a blue cube below your first pattern so that you have red, blue, red, blue. Describe the pattern and then ask

  "What color cube do I put next?"
  "¿De qué color será el siguiente cubo?"

- If the child does not recognize that red comes next, begin at the top and touch and name each cube.

  "Red. Blue. (pause) Red. Blue."
  "Rojo. Azul. (Pausa) Rojo. Azul."

  Have the child touch the cubes and name the colors.

- Continue repeating the pattern until the child can make and describe the pattern.
- Change colors and repeat the procedure several times. You may use two blocks that are the same color.
- Let the child initiate a pattern for you to reproduce.

LEVELS OF EXPERIENCE

- Use other objects or pictures of objects that vary only in color.

- Let the child use colored stars to make repeating vertical patterns. Encourage the child to see how tall he/she can make the pattern string.
- Let the child use pattern cards as models for repeating patterns.

- Pair children and let them take turns initiating, copying, and repeating patterns.
- Stacking blocks is a fun way to repeat vertical patterns. See who can make the tallest tower of the repeating pattern.

Two Objects by Shape
Dos objetos por forma

Primary Skills & Concepts

One-to-one correspondence, visual discrimination,
left-to-right progression, sequence

Materials

Parquetry blocks or shapes cut from paper or felt

KEEP IN MIND

- This activity is limited to patterns of two objects with one variable—shape.

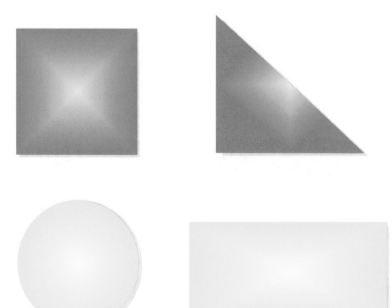

Patterning 5- HORIZONTAL

Primary Activity

- Choose several parquetry blocks that are the same color but different shapes. (We'll use red squares and triangles.) Tell the child that you are going to make a pattern. From the child's left to right display a red square, saying

  "My pattern starts on your left. First, I'll use a square. Next, I'll use a triangle. This is my pattern. Square. Triangle."

  "Mi patrón empieza por la izquierda. Primero pongo un cuadrado. El siguiente es un triángulo. Este es mi patrón. Cuadrado. Triángulo."

- Make and describe the pattern again directly below the first pattern. Then ask the child to make the pattern. If the child does not describe the pattern as he/she makes it, you describe it. Continue until the child can make and describe the pattern.
- Change shapes and repeat the procedure several times. You may use two blocks that are the same shape.
- Let the child initiate a pattern for you to reproduce.

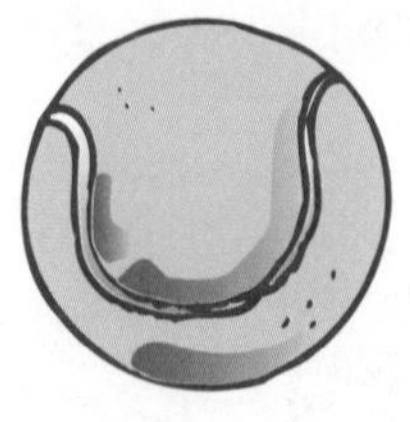
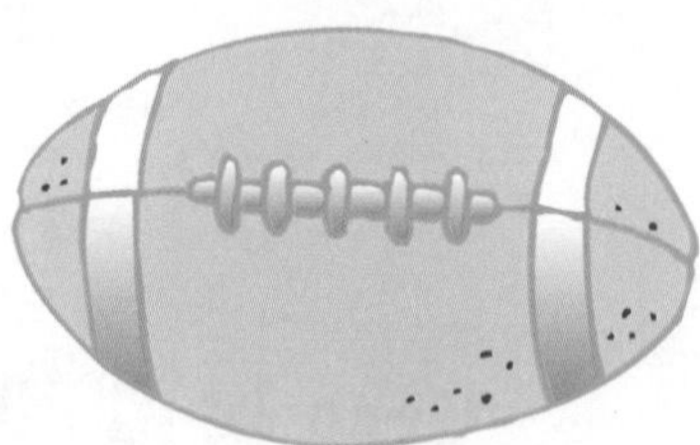

LEVELS OF EXPERIENCE

- Use other objects or pictures of objects that vary only in shape; for example, round blue button/square blue buttons, round red beads/square red beads, or round crackers/square crackers.

- Make pattern cards. Draw shape patterns on index cards. Put them in a learning center with the parquetry blocks so the child can work independently.

- Make patterns of shape stickers (blue stars, blue circles) for the child to reproduce.
- Cut out and color pictures of theme-related shapes for the children to use in patterning. Make pattern cards to go with the shapes. For example, you might make orange leaves/orange pumpkins or red bears/red dinosaurs.

Repeating Two Objects by Shape
Repetir dos objetos por forma

Primary Skills & Concepts

One-to-one correspondence, visual discrimination, left-to-right progression, sequence

Materials

Parquetry blocks or shapes cut from paper or felt

KEEP IN MIND

- Repeating a two-item pattern is a logical extension of the Level 5 activity.

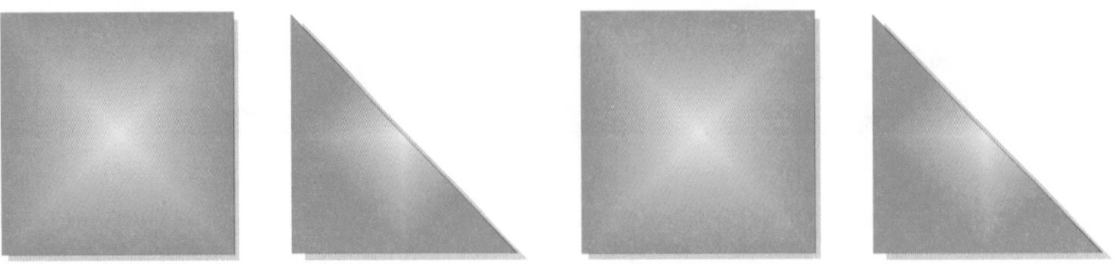

Patterning 6- Horizontal

Primary Activity

- From the child's left to right display a red square, saying

  "My pattern starts on your left. First, I'll use a square. Next, I'll use a triangle. This is my pattern. Square. Triangle. Now I'm going to make my pattern again."

  "Mi patrón empieza por la izquierda. Primero, pongo un cuadrado. El siguiente será un triángulo. Este es mi patrón. Cuadrado. Triángulo. Ahora voy a volver a hacer mi patrón."
- Place a red square and then a red triangle next to your first pattern so that you have square, triangle, square, triangle. Describe the pattern and then ask

  "What shape do I put next?"

  "¿Qué forma debe ser la siguiente?"
- If the child does not recognize that square comes next, begin at the child's left and touch and name each shape.

  "Square. Triangle. (pause) Square. Triangle."

  "Cuadrado. Triángulo. (Pausa) Cuadrado. Triángulo."

  Have the child touch the items and name the shapes.
- Continue repeating the pattern until the child can make and describe the pattern.
- Change shapes and repeat the procedure several times. You may use two blocks that are the same shape.
- Let the child initiate a pattern for you to reproduce.

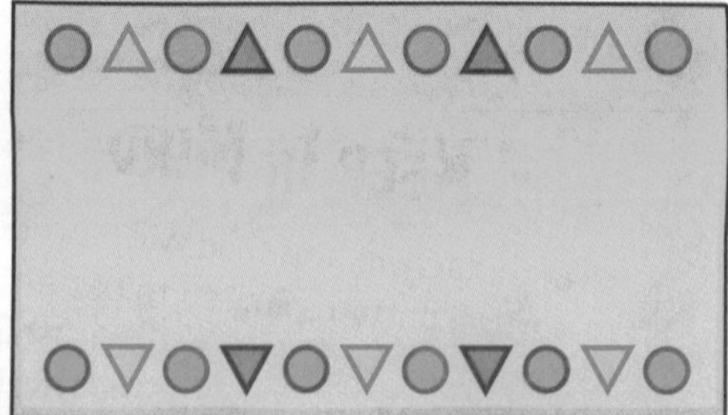

Levels Of Experience

- Use other objects or pictures of objects that vary only in shape.
- Let the child string beads of different shapes in patterns.

- Encourage the child to see how long he/she can make the pattern string.
- Use pattern cards as models for repeating patterns.
- Pair children and let them take turns initiating, copying, and repeating patterns.

- Give the child shapes cut from paper to arrange in patterns and paste to another sheet of paper.
- Let the children make place mats with repeating patterns as decoration.
- Let the children make bulletin board borders of repeating shape patterns.

Two Objects by Shape
Dos objetos por forma

Primary Skills & Concepts

One-to-one correspondence, shape discrimination, top-to-bottom progression, sequence

Materials

Parquetry blocks or shapes cut from paper or felt

KEEP IN MIND

- In this activity the child will reproduce vertical patterns limited to patterns of two objects with one variable—shape. It is basically the same as the Level 5 activity, but the orientation is changed.

Primary Activity

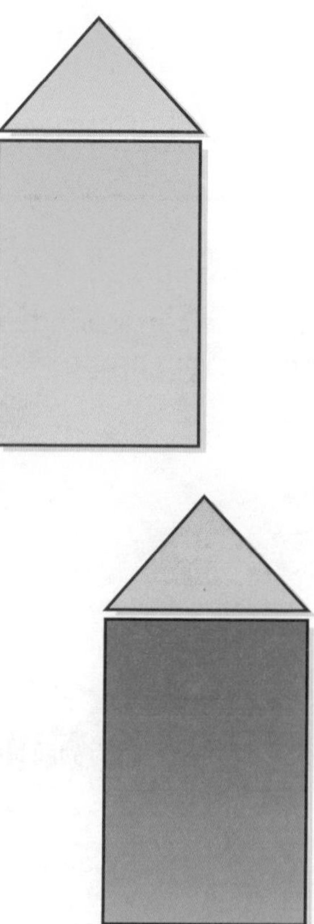

- Choose several parquetry blocks in two shapes. (We'll use blue squares and triangles.) Tell the child that you are going to make a pattern. Display a blue square, saying

  "My pattern starts here. First, I'll use a square. Next, I'll use a triangle. I put the triangle below the square. This is my pattern. It goes from top to bottom. Square. Triangle."
  "Mi patrón empieza aquí. Primero pongo un cuadrado. El siguiente es un triángulo. Pongo el triángulo bajo el cuadrado. Este es mi patrón. Va desde la parte de arriba a la parte de abajo. Cuadrado. Triángulo."

- Make and describe the pattern again directly beside the first pattern. Then ask the child to make the pattern. If the child does not describe the pattern as he/she makes it, you describe it. Continue until the child can make and describe the pattern.
- Change shapes and repeat the procedure several times. You may use two blocks that are the same shape.
- Let the child initiate a pattern for you to reproduce.

LEVELS OF EXPERIENCE

- Use other objects or pictures of objects that vary only in shape.

- Make pattern cards. Draw shape patterns on index cards. Put them in a learning center with the parquetry blocks so the child can work independently.
- Make patterns of colored stars and circles for the child to reproduce.

- Cut out and color pictures of theme-related items for the children to use in patterning. Make pattern cards to go with the shapes.

Patterning 8- VERTICAL

Repeating Two Objects by Shape
Repetir dos objetos por forma

Primary Skills & Concept

One-to-one correspondence, visual discrimination, top-to-bottom progression, sequence

Materials

Parquetry blocks or shapes cut from paper or felt

KEEP IN MIND

- This is basically the same as the Level 6 activity, but the orientation is changed.

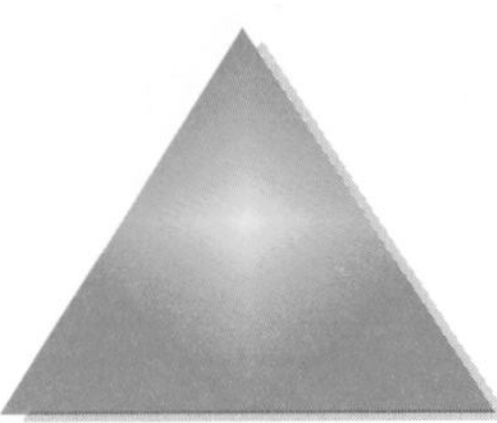

Patterning 8- VERTICAL

Primary Activity

- Display a red square, saying

  "My pattern starts here. First, I'll use a square. Next, I'll use a triangle. I put the triangle below the square. This is my pattern. Square. Triangle. Now I'm going make my pattern again."

  "Mi patrón empieza aquí. Primero pongo un cuadrado. El siguiente será un triángulo. Pongo el triángulo debajo del cuadrado. Este es mi patrón. Cuadrado. Triángulo. Ahora voy a volver a hacer mi patrón."

- Place a square and then a triangle below your first pattern so that you have square, triangle, square, triangle. Describe the pattern and then ask

  "What shape do I put next?"

  "¿Qué forma debe ser la siguiente?"

- If the child does not recognize that the square comes next, begin at the top and touch and name each shape.

  "Square. Triangle. (pause) Square. Triangle."

  "Cuadrado. Triángulo. (pausa) Cuadrado. Triángulo."

  Have the child touch the items and name the shapes.

- Continue repeating the pattern until the child can make and describe the pattern.
- Change shapes and repeat the procedure several times. You may use two blocks that are the same shape.
- Let the child initiate a pattern for you to reproduce.

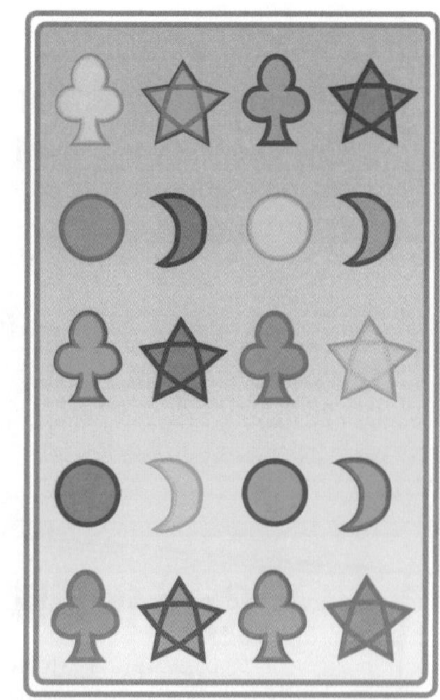

LEVELS OF EXPERIENCE

- Use other objects or pictures of objects that vary only in shape.

Let the child use colored stars and circles to make repeating vertical patterns. Encourage the child to see how tall he/she can make the pattern.

- Let the child use pattern cards as models for repeating patterns.
- Pair children and let them take turns initiating, copying, and repeating patterns.
- Give the children cookie cutters in two shapes and let them cut out clay cookies and arrange them in repeating patterns on a cookie sheet.

By Color and Shape
Por color y forma

Primary Skills & Concepts

One-to-one correspondence, visual discrimination, color discrimination, left-to-right progression, top-to-bottom progression, sequence

Materials

Similar objects with two variables such as red and blue cubes and red and blue beads, cut paper or felt squares and triangles in two colors

Keep In Mind

- In this activity the children will be identifying and reproducing patterns using objects with two variables—color and shape.

Patterning 9- Two Variables

Primary Activity

- Tell the child that you are going to make a pattern. From the child's left to right display a red cube, saying

  "My pattern starts on your left. First, I'll use a red cube. Next, I'll use a blue bead. This is my pattern. Red cube. Blue bead."

  "Mi patrón empieza por la izquierda. Primero pongo un cubo rojo. El siguiente será una cuenta azul. Este es mi patrón. Cubo rojo. Cuenta azul."
- Make and describe the pattern again directly below the first pattern. Then ask the child to make the pattern. If the child does not describe the pattern as he/she makes it, you describe it. Continue until the child can make and describe the pattern.
- Change colors and shapes and repeat the procedure several times.
- Let the child initiate a pattern for you to reproduce.
- Repeat the procedure with a vertical pattern.

Levels Of Experience

- Extend the number of items in the pattern to three, using just two variables.
- Provide sponges cut into geometric shapes and tempera paint for the child to use in making a pattern at the top of a sheet of paper. Then have the child reproduce the pattern again and again below the original pattern.

- Let the child use pegs and a pegboard to create and reproduce patterns.
- Let the children work in pairs with pegs and pegboards or blocks to initiate and reproduce patterns.

- Help the children look for and identify patterns any time you work with them. Among other things, they will learn to recognize letter patterns in print, tone and beat patterns in music, decorative patterns in insects and animals, bead patterns in necklaces, design patterns in fabrics, and even patterns in daily routines.

Patterning 10- Two Variables

Repeating by Color and Shape
Repetir por color y forma

Primary Skills & Concepts

One-to-one correspondence, visual discrimination, color discrimination, left-to-right progression, top-to-bottom progression, sequence

Materials

Similar objects with two variables such as red and blue cubes and red and blue beads, cut paper or felt squares and triangles in two colors

Primary Activity

- From the child's left to right display a red cube, saying

  "My pattern starts on your left. First, I'll use a red cube. Next, I'll use a blue bead. This is my pattern. Red cube. Blue bead. Now I'm going to make my pattern again."
  "Mi patrón empieza por la izquierda. Primero pongo un cubo rojo. El siguiente será una cuenta azul. Así es mi patrón. Cubo rojo. Cuenta azul. Ahora voy a volver a hacer mi patrón."

- Place a red cube and then a blue bead next to your first pattern so that you have red cube, blue bead, red cube, blue bead. Describe the pattern and then ask

  "What do I put next?"
  "¿Qué es lo siguiente que debo poner?"

- If the child does not recognize that red cube comes next, begin at the child's left and touch and name each item.

  "Red cube. Blue bead. (pause) Red cube. Blue bead."
  "Cubo rojo. Cuenta azul. (Pausa) Cubo rojo. Cuenta azul."

  Have the child touch the cubes and beads and name the colors.

- Continue repeating the pattern until the child can make and describe the pattern.
- Change colors and shapes and repeat the procedure several times.
- Let the child initiate a pattern for you to reproduce.
- Repeat the procedure with a vertical pattern.

Levels Of Experience

- Extend the number of items in the pattern to three, using just two variables.

- Provide sponges cut into geometric shapes and tempera paint for the child to use in making a pattern down the left side of a sheet of paper. Then have the child reproduce the pattern again and again to the right of the original pattern.

- Let the child use pegs and a pegboard to create and reproduce patterns.
- Let the children work in pairs with pegs and pegboards or blocks to initiate and reproduce patterns.

Creeping & Crawling
Andar a gatas & deslizarse

Primary Skills & Concepts

Spatial and directional awareness, flexibility, movement of body parts

Materials

Carpeted or padded floor

KEEP IN MIND

- Physical education deals with the child's ability to move in relation to his/her environment.
- Although most four- and five-year-old children have acquired basic motor skills, their skill level is often low in many areas. Physical education provides a structured method for developing and refining skills, and repeated practice develops proficiency and retention.
- Motor control and physical activity are essential elements of a healthy mental and physical life.
- Children should practice these motor skills hundreds of times. So, use these activity suggestions as models for other activities.
- Always demonstrate and describe your movements so the child will know what is expected and can concentrate on improving.

Gross Motor Movement 1 - Creeping & Crawling

Primary Activity

- At the basic level, the child lies face down on the floor with his/her head and chest raised. The child reaches forward with both arms and pulls forward without using his/her legs. Then the child crawls on his/her hands and knees by moving one arm/leg at a time in a left arm/right knee/right arm/left knee pattern, pausing between movements.
- At the highest level, the child crawls smoothly by moving opposing arms and legs at the same time.

Levels Of Experience

- For most children, crawling is boring unless it is part of a game. Turn crawling into a race: let three or four children crawl while pushing a box or block with their chins.
- Relate the crawling activity to a theme. Let the children pretend to be four-legged dinosaurs roaming around the forest or swamp calling out to each other with their best dinosaur voices.
- Let the children crawl to music, moving slowly, quickly, and stopping when the music stops.
- Have the children crawl around and under obstacles such as chairs and tables as they search for hidden treasures.

Posture
Correctamente

Primary Skills & Concepts

Spatial and directional awareness, balance

Materials

Vertical tape line on a full-length mirror or plumb line from the ceiling

Keep in Mind

- It is common belief that proper posture allows our organs and muscles to function more efficiently, and it is certainly more attractive than poor posture. Poor posture is often an indication that a person is suffering from physical or emotional stress, and we tend to think of poor posture as a sign of laziness and lethargy.
- You can help your children develop good posture without constantly nagging if you periodically remind them to "think tall."

Primary Activity

- You can check posture by having the child stand with his/her side to the tape or plumb line. Think of an imaginary line drawn from the center top of the head down the edge of the shoulder, past the hip bone, behind the kneecap, to the center of the foot.
- When standing properly, the

  feet will be about six inches apart and parallel.

  head will be held high with the chin parallel to the floor.

  chest will be out.

  stomach will be flat.

  knees will be slightly bent, not locked.

  weight will be distributed evenly with most on the balls of the feet.

Levels Of Experience

- Use the age-old trick of standing with a lightweight book balanced on the head.

- Most children are aware that people who think they are important carry themselves differently than the rest of us. You might ask them to stand as though they were kings/queens, the president, or a movie star.

  Actúen como si fueran un/a rey/reina, el presidente o una estrella de cine.

- To help emphasize the difference between poor and proper standing posture, ask the children to show how people stand when they are very sad.

  Párense y pónganse tristes.

- Talk about the positions of the head, arms, shoulders, back. Then ask them to show how people stand when they have done something wonderful or very important and discuss the differences.

  Muestren como se pararían si hubieran hecho algo bueno o importante. ¿Cuál es la diferencia?

Posture
Correctamente

Primary Skills & Concepts

Spatial and directional awareness, balance

Materials

Chair

Primary Activity

- Have the child sit so that his/her hips touch the back of the chair. If the child is "sitting tall" "sentado/a derecho/a," the back will naturally curve slightly at the waist. Make sure the child holds his/her chest out and keeps his/her neck on a line with the spine. Feet should be flat on the floor. (Crossing our legs is comfortable for a short time, but it does slow circulation in our legs and feet.) When the child is writing or drawing, he/she should lean forward from the hips and keep the head and shoulders in line.

LEVELS OF EXPERIENCE

- One way to check sitting posture is to place a pencil or ruler on the child's shoulder. If he/she is "slumping," the pencil/ruler will fall off.

Balance and Flexibility
Equilibrio y flexibilidad

Primary Skills & Concepts

Spatial and directional awareness, posture, awareness of body parts, movement of body parts, imitating movement

Materials

Chair

KEEP IN MIND

- As you've noticed, young children seem to have a great deal of difficulty sitting in a chair and purposefully moving body parts at the same time. By the time a child is four-years-old, this probably has more to do with lack of concentration and general "wiggliness" than anything else. However, practice can help in both areas.

Primary Activity

- At the lowest level, the child should be able to sit and point to body parts as directed. Have the child sit in a chair, using proper posture. Name a body part and ask the child to point to it. The child returns to the original position before pointing to another body part. Demonstrate as you give directions to help the child learn and remember the names of body parts.
- At the next level, the child moves body parts while sitting. Give the child directions for moving and demonstrate.
  "Raise your hands above your head."
  "Levanten las manos sobre la cabeza."
  You will notice that you are also reinforcing position words in this activity.

Levels Of Experience

- Do both of the activities to music.
- Play Simon Says while sitting.
- Have the children stomp, march, and swing their feet while sitting in a chair.

Balance and Flexibility
Equilibrio y flexibilidad

Primary Skills & Concepts

Spatial and directional awareness, posture, awareness of body parts, movement of body parts, imitating movement

Materials

None

KEEP IN MIND

- When a child has posture control, he/she is able to maintain balance whether static or moving.
- When he/she has posture flexibility, the child is able to regain posture ontrol after moving.
- At this point, we will deal with balance and flexibility in the standing position only.
- Begin at the lowest level and work with the children until they have mastered it. Then move on to the next level.

Gross Motor Movement 5 - Standing

Primary Activity

- At the lowest level, the child should be able to stand and point to body parts as directed. Have the child stand, using proper posture. Name a body part and ask the child to point to it. The child returns to the original position before pointing to another body part. If you demonstrate as you give directions, you will be helping the child learn and remember the names of body parts.
- At the next level, the child moves body parts while standing in place. Have the child stand, using proper posture. Give the child directions for moving and demonstrate.
  "Raise your hands above your head."
  "Levanten las manos sobre la cabeza."
- The third level deals with moving in space while standing. Give directions that require the child to move body parts forward, backward, and sideways. Some children will need to hold onto a chair or wall to help themselves balance when they are standing on one foot.
- Raise the third level by having the child hold a position while balancing on one leg from five to ten seconds as you count slowly.

Levels Of Experience

- Vary and extend each level of these activities by having the child move in different levels of space: with knees bent and on tiptoe.
- Use only visual signs to indicate how the child is to move.

- Play Simon Says.
- Let a child lead the activities.
- Let children move with scarves or streamers.
- Do the movements to music.

- Let the children perform on a low balance beam.
- Let the children randomly move body parts while standing in place. When you say "Freeze," "¡No se muevan!" the children hold their poses. The one who holds his/her pose longest gets to be the next leader. Count slowly as the children freeze.
- *For higher level activities, see Imitating Movements.*

On a Level Surface
Sobre una superficie plana

Primary Skills & Concepts

Spatial and directional awareness, posture, awareness of body parts, movement of body parts, balance, flexibility

Materials

None

KEEP IN MIND

- When children begin walking, they move flat-footed with their legs far apart and they lean forward and raise their arms and legs in an attempt to move and balance at the same time.
- As they mature, they begin to swing their arms slightly and in opposition to the legs. The posture is more upright and they begin using the heel-toe pattern.
- Most four-years-olds are able to walk in the heel-toe pattern while swinging their arms in opposition to their legs.
- As the children walk, you will notice some common faults. If they push off too hard, they will bounce. If their toes are turned out, they will "duck walk." If their toes are turned in, they appear "pigeon-toed."

Gross Motor Movement 6 – Walking

Primary Activity

- Beginning from the standing posture, have the children walk freely as you watch and demonstrate changes. Then have them walk forward and backward.
- Let them experiment with walking with their toes turned out, in, and straight ahead and with their legs stiff.
- Have them change speed as they walk. As speed increases, the stride will get longer.

Levels Of Experience

- Let the children practice walking with their knees held high.
- Have the children walk with very long steps, like giants, and very small steps, like elves.
- Pair the children and let them walk in a variety of ways holding hands with their partner.
- Use a drum or metronome to keep time, and let the children walk to the beat.
- Let the children walk through an obstacle course of tables, chairs, and ropes.

On a Sloping Surface
Sobre una superficie inclinada

Primary Skills & Concepts

Spatial and directional awareness, posture, awareness of body parts, movement of body parts, balance, flexibility

Materials

Ramp

Getting Ready

- Use a building access ramp or make a ramp with a sheet of plywood and bricks.

Primary Activity

- When walking up a slope, the child shifts the center of gravity by leaning forward. When going down, the child leans back. The lean should be from the ankles, not from the waist.
- As the children practice walking up and down the ramp, some will need to hold your hand. Gradually decrease your support as skill develops.

LEVELS OF EXPERIENCE

- Gradually increase the angle of the ramp.

- Let the children walk backward up and down the ramp while holding your hand or a handrail.

- Have the children walk up and down the ramp with a partner.
- Take the children outside and let them walk up and down small hills.

Marching
Desfilar

Primary Skills & Concepts

Spatial and directional awareness, posture, awareness of body parts, movement of body parts, balance, flexibility

Materials

None

KEEP IN MIND

- In order to march, a child must be able to balance for short periods on one leg and raise his/her knees higher than in a normal walk. The arms may be at the child's sides or held up and bent.

Primary Activity

- Begin by having the child march in place. Demonstrate each step. Have the child stand with proper posture, then raise one knee high enough that the heel is about midcalf on the opposing leg. Lower the leg and raise the other knee. When the child understands the pattern, count the march steps 1 . . . 2 . . . 1 . . . 2. As the child gets used to marching, he/she will begin moving the opposing arms in rhythm.
- When the children can march well in place, let them march around the room. At the early stages, let them march randomly. Later you can have them march in a line or in a circle.

LEVELS OF EXPERIENCE

- Have the children raise their legs higher as they march.
- Change speed by changing the speed of counting or beating the drum.
- Let the children march to music.

Up and Down Steps
Subir y bajar escalones

Primary Skills & Concepts

Spatial and directional awareness, posture, awareness of body parts, movement of body parts, balance, flexibility

Materials

Steps

KEEP IN MIND

- In order to successfully deal with steps, a child must be able to walk and balance for a few seconds on one leg. Walking up steps also requires that he/she raise the knees higher than in a normal walk.
- When children begin climbing stairs, they pause with both feet on each step and lead with the dominant leg. Often they will begin climbing stairs by facing the handrail and moving up and down sideways. Some of this is lack of coordination and some is that adult-size steps are too tall for short children to climb easily while maintaining balance.
- Marching is good training for using stairs.

Getting Ready

- You will need a single step and stairs with at least three or four steps. For the single step, you can use a sturdy wooden box about 3" high and big enough for a child to stand on comfortably.

Primary Activity

- Begin by using a single step. Always demonstrate, and, if necessary, walk with the child. Have the child stand near the step in proper standing posture. Beginning with the dominant leg, the child raises the knee high enough that the foot clears the step, moves the leg forward, and lowers the foot onto the step. Leaning forward slightly for balance, and holding your hand or a handrail if necessary, the child lifts the back foot, raises it, pulls it forward, and places it on the step beside the other foot.
- The child should go down the step forward to begin with. He/she lifts the dominant leg to clear the step, leans forward slightly for balance, and lowers the dominant leg to the floor. Then the child raises the back foot, pulls it forward, and lowers it to the floor beside the other foot. Have the child repeat this many times.
- When the children can climb three or four steps using the step-step-pause pattern with no trouble, encourage them to continue moving.

  "Raise one leg. Put it on the next step. Raise the other leg. Put it on the next step."
  "Levanten una pierna, pónganla en el siguiente escalón Levanten la otra pierna, pónganla en el siguiente escalón."

  Always be ready to offer your hand for balance.
- Coming down, most children will use a handrail, the wall, or your hand for balance. Again, most beginners will pause at each step and lead off with the dominant leg. Help them move smoothly by saying
  "Raise your knee. Push your leg out. Lower your foot to the next step. Raise your other knee. Push your leg out. Lower your foot to the next step."
  "Levanten la rodilla. Estiren la pierna. Pongan el pie en el siguiente escalón. Levanten la otra rodilla. Estiren la pierna. Pongan el pie en el siguiente escalón."

Levels Of Experience

- Use steps as part of everyday routines. For example, when a child is sharing during circle time, he/she can stand at the top of the stair. Put steps near the drinking fountain and sink.
- Add steps to your obstacle course for walking.

Bending
Doblar

Primary Skills & Concepts

Spatial and directional awareness, posture, awareness of body parts, movement of body parts, balance, flexibility

Materials

None

Keep In Mind

- Bending, movement of two bones around a joint, and stretching, extension of a joint, often go together. Some actions require several bending movements.
- The extent of bending and stretching a child can do depends in part on flexibility.
- Bending and stretching are essential to all action.
- We will deal first with bending that does not require hyperextension. Bending with hyperextension is covered under Stretching.
- Work on one or two activities for a few minutes each day.

Primary Activity

- Begin by working on bending large body parts such as the limbs. Demonstrate and describe each movement as you do it with the children. In the standing posture, have the child stand with arms next to the body, palms forward. Bend the arms at the elbow straight up toward the shoulders. Do it slowly and gradually increase the speed.
- Have the child stand with arms outstretched, palms up. Bend the arms at the elbows and touch the shoulders, slowly and then quickly.
- Rotate the arms so the palms are down. Bend the arms at the elbows, slowly and quickly. With the arms hanging down, swing the lower arms slowly.
- In the standing posture, slowly bend the knees forward and down slightly. Gradually increase the extent of the bend. Knees are not designed for "deep" bends so don't have the children do repeated deep knee bends.
- From the standing posture, slowly bend forward and down at the waist. Gradually increase the depth of the bend. Do the same thing with sideward bends.
- Holding onto the wall or a handrail, stand on one leg. Bend the other knee up, bend the foot up at the ankle, bend the foot down at the ankle, lower the leg.

LEVELS OF EXPERIENCE

- Do bending exercises to music.

- Combine arm and knee bends. Remember that young children can remember only two or three commands at one time.
- Walk while bending at the waist.

- Walk while bending at the knee.
- Do bending activities while lying on the floor.

Stretching
Estirarse

Primary Skills & Concepts

Spatial and directional awareness, posture, awareness of body parts, movement of body parts, balance, flexibility

Materials

None

KEEP IN MIND

- Stretching is the extension or hyperextension of joints. It is part of most daily tasks and most sports.
- Before practicing stretching exercises, warm up with bending and walking activities. It will help children to name something to reach for as they stretch.
- Repeat two or three activities several times each day.

Primary Activity

- From the standing posture, raise arms and hands above the head and reach up for the (ceiling). With arms outstretched, reach out for the (walls).
- Bend forward at the waist and reach for the toes. Do not bounce. With feet 6" to 12" apart, bend forward at the waist and reach for the toes.
- Lying down, raise one leg and reach for the (ceiling.) Repeat with the other leg.
- Sitting on the floor, stretch legs to the front and reach for the (wall) with toes. Spread legs apart and reach.

LEVELS OF EXPERIENCE

- Stretch to music.
- Pretend to be a rubber band and stretch as far as you can.

- Stretch one arm while bending the other.
- Stretch one leg while bending the other.

- Stretch neck, fingers, and toes.
- Combine bends and stretches.

Imitating Movements
Imitar movimientos

Primary Skills & Concepts

Spatial and directional awareness, posture, awareness of body parts, movement of body parts, balance, flexibility

Materials

None

KEEP IN MIND

- You may use any actions that are familiar to the children at this point. Later, as the children develop and refine additional gross motor movements, add them to the activities.

Primary Activity

- Begin imitating by standing in front of the children with your back to them. You will need to turn your head, of course, so you can watch them. Perform one action while describing what you are doing and then have the children repeat the action with you as you repeat the directions. Do the same action several times before changing to a different action.
- When the children are able to imitate a simple action with oral directions, perform simple actions without oral directions. Again, do one action at a time.
- Combine two actions. Perform the actions while describing them and then have the children repeat the actions with you as you repeat the directions.
- Follow the same procedures while you are facing the children.
- Let children take turns leading the group.
- Group the children into pairs. Let one be the leader and the other the mirror.

Levels Of Experience

- Do the activities to appropriate music.
- Play Follow the Leader or Simon Says.
- Let the children try following your oral directions with their eyes closed.

Pulling
Jalar

Primary Skills & Concepts

Spatial and directional awareness, posture, awareness of body parts, movement of body parts, balance, flexibility

Materials

Small objects such as blocks, pencils, small boxes
Heavier objects with handles such as tubs, wagons, boxes

KEEP IN MIND

- Pulling, drawing an object toward the body, is usually done with the muscles of the arms and back.
- When an object is heavy, the legs can supply additional force. Pulling is an action used daily in work and play.
- Do pulling exercises with light objects. As children develop strength, increase the weight of the objects.

Gross Motor Movement 13 - Pulling

Primary Activity

- Pulling begins with the arms extended. As the child draws the object toward himself/herself, the elbows and wrists bend. If the child is standing to pull, pulling begins with knees bent and as the object moves toward the body, the back and knees straighten.
- Begin with the child sitting at a table. Place a small object at arm's length from the child. Have the child pull the object toward himself/herself using one hand. If the child must lean, have him/her lean from the waist.
- Increase the weight of the objects until the child must pull with two hands.
- Place a light-weight object on the floor about arm's length from the child. The child will squat or bend and reach out. As he/she pulls the object toward himself/herself, the child will bend his/her arms and straighten his/her back. Do not let the child bend at the waist to pull a heavy object.

Levels Of Experience

- Pull an object from the back of the body (a wagon, pull toy, box with a string handle) and from the side.
- Walk while pulling something from behind.
- Walk backward while pulling something from in front.
- Pull an object while kneeling or lying on the floor.
- Vary speed while pulling.
- Play Tug-of-War.

Pushing
Empujar

Primary Skills & Concepts

Spatial and directional awareness, posture, awareness of body parts, movement of body parts, balance, flexibility

Materials

Small objects such as blocks, pencils, small boxes
Heavier objects such as tubs, boxes, chairs

Keep In Mind

- Pushing is basically opposite to pulling. The movement is away from the body and against an object.
- Depending on the force required, pushing is done with legs, arms, feet, shoulders, hips, or a combination. Unless the object is tall, the child must bend or stoop to push it.

Gross Motor Movement 14 - Pushing

Primary Activity

- While the child is sitting at a table, place a small object in front of him/her—close enough that he/she will have to bend his/her elbow and wrist. Have the child place one hand against the object and push it by extending the arm until it is straight. Children should practice pushing with both the dominant and the nondominant hand.
- Give the child increasingly heavier objects until he/she is pushing with both hands.
- Have the child push objects on the floor. Depending on the height and weight of the object, the child will have to bend, stoop, or crawl on his/her knees while pushing with his/her hands.
- Have the child sit on the floor and push objects with his/her feet.
- Have the child stand and push objects with his/her feet. This is not kicking. The object being pushed will not leave the ground and the pushing motion is smooth and continuous.

Levels of Experience

- To help the child develop control while pushing, designate specific distances for the child to push.

  "Push your pencil to my hand."

  "Empuja ese lápiz hacia mí."

- Push with the back against an object.
- Begin lying face down and push off the floor with hands.

- Pair the children. The pairs lie on the floor with the soles of their feet together and push.

Swinging
Balancear

Primary Skills & Concepts

Spatial and directional awareness, posture, awareness of body parts, movement of body parts, balance, flexibility, pushing, pulling

Materials

None

KEEP IN MIND

- With young children, limit swinging to the arms and legs.
- In a swing, the body part is allowed to drop into space and the force of the drop carries the part upward. Increasing the force of the drop, increases the speed of the swing and carries it further. With enough force, the body part will swing up and over making a full circle.

Primary Activity

- Begin in the standing posture. As you demonstrate, describe what you're doing. Hold one arm straight out in front of your body parallel to the ground. Let the arm drop and don't stop the motion. Repeat several times and then change arms and repeat.
- Follow the same procedure with the legs. Initially, most children will need to balance by placing the opposing hand on a wall, handrail, chair, or table.
- After the child is comfortable with the "drop swing," have her/him add force to the arm drop so the swing will continue up and over. You might want to help by moving the child's arm for him/her until he/she feels the movement.

LEVELS OF EXPERIENCE

- Swing continuously with a slow, smooth motion. Gradually increase the speed of the swing.
- Swing one arm forward while swinging the other arm backward.
- Swing scarves and streamers.

- Swing one arm and the opposite leg.
- Pair the children and let the partners mirror each other's swings.

- When the children have learned to apply force to their swings, you can let them try swinging an arm or leg across their body. This will be difficult for most four-year-olds to do without twisting their bodies as they swing because most are not ready to cross the body's midline. The child begins with the arm outstretched to the side and moves it across his/her body. This involves pushing and pulling at the same time.
- Pair the children and let them swing ropes, one child on each end of a rope.

Turning
Girar

Primary Skills & Concepts

Spatial and directional awareness, posture, awareness of body parts, movement of body parts, balance, flexibility, pushing, pulling

Materials

None

Keep in Mind

- Twisting and turning are closely related actions, and we will work with them in their simplest terms. Think of a turn as a rotation in space. A turn can continue without the body part having to move backward to the original position. You can turn your entire body: face forward and move your entire body continuously to the left or right. You can turn your body partway—a quarter turn, a half turn.
- On the other hand a twist is a forward and backward rotation of the body or body part on its own axis. The body part cannot turn 360° and it must move backward to its original position. From the shoulder you can twist your arm nearly 180°. From the wrist you can twist your hand just a few degrees without also twisting your arm.
- The simplest turn is to face forward and move the entire body in a circle. When this is done quickly, we call it a spin, and the force required to stop the turning is greater.

Primary Activity

- Have the child sit on the floor and turn his/her body.
- Have the child lie on his/her stomach on the floor and turn—the stomach is the pivot point.
- Have the child lie on his/her back and turn—the middle of the back is the pivot point.

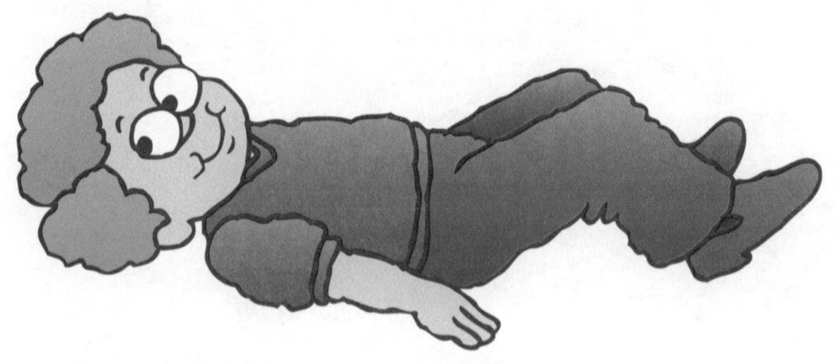

LEVELS OF EXPERIENCE

- Vary the rate of turning

- Turn around a chair.
- Turn around a partner.

- Move around the room while turning.

Twisting
Torcer

Primary Skills & Concepts

Spatial and directional awareness, posture, awareness of body parts, movement of body parts, balance, flexibility, pushing, pulling

Materials

None

Keep in Mind

- A twist is a forward and backward rotation of the body or body part on its own axis. The body part cannot turn 360° and it must move backward to its original position. The spine, neck, shoulder, hip, and wrist joints are the only places where twisting can take place.
- From the shoulder you can twist your arm nearly 180°. Think of using a screwdriver: from the wrist you can twist your hand just a few degrees without also twisting your arm. Your wrist and arm must return to the original position before you can continue using the screwdriver.

Primary Activity

- Have the children begin by simply twisting their heads from left to right.
- Have them extend their arms and twist them. Then twist just the wrist.
- Have the children twist their legs.
- Have the children stand with their hands on their hips and twist at the hip.

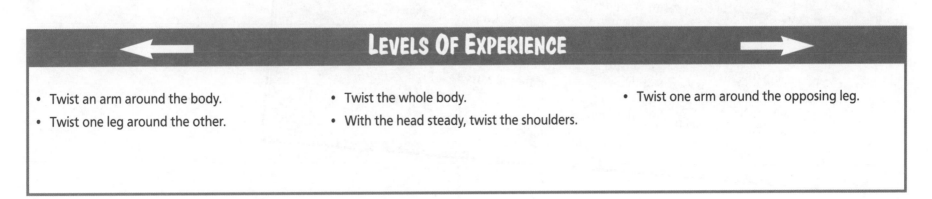

Levels Of Experience

- Twist an arm around the body.
- Twist one leg around the other.

- Twist the whole body.
- With the head steady, twist the shoulders.

- Twist one arm around the opposing leg.

Running & Stopping
Correr y detenerse

Primary Skills & Concepts

Spatial and directional awareness, posture, awareness of body parts, movement of body parts, balance, flexibility, pushing, pulling, endurance

Materials

None

KEEP IN MIND

- Running is similar to walking; however, there is a period during which both feet are off the ground. Weight should be taken on the ball of the foot. The knees are bent more and move upward and forward while the arms are bent at the elbows and move in opposition to the legs. The body leans forward.
- The beginning runner runs flat-footed with feet far apart and the legs bent slightly. (It's not bulky diapers that cause this running form, it's an attempt to balance.) As running ability improves, the arms drop below the waist, the legs bend at about 90°, and the stride is the heel-to-toe pattern.
- When stopping, the feet are in the forward position, the knees are bent, and the body leans backward and balances.
- As you demonstrate, always use the mature running form—the children need a good model if they are to develop.

Primary Activity

- Begin by having the children run in place. This will help them establish the relationship between the legs and arms and will help them establish a balanced stance. Start slowly and gradually build speed.
- Draw a line about ten feet from the child and have him/her run to the line and stop. Gradually move the line farther from the child.
- Have the child run and stop on a signal.

LEVELS OF EXPERIENCE

- Run in a circle.
- Play Follow the Leader and include running.

- Play tag. Divide the group into pairs. One partner starts running on a signal. The other starts on a second signal and tries to tag the first partner.

- Play Squirrels in the Tree. Divide the class into groups of four. Two children will stand facing each other with the hands joined above their heads to form a tree. The third and fourth child are squirrels. The trees form a large circle, the squirrels stand in the center of the circle. When you say "Run, squirrels, run" "¡A correr ardillitas!" the squirrels run to a tree and sit under it—only one squirrel to a tree. Then have the children change positions and play again.

Vertical
Hacia arriba

Primary Skills & Concepts

Spatial and directional awareness, posture, awareness of body parts, movement of body parts, balance, flexibility, pushing, pulling

Materials

None

Keep In Mind

- The jumping motion carries the body through the air, suspends it momentarily, and drops it to the ground. The takeoff and landing can be one-footed or two-footed.
- Children begin jumping by pushing off from a step or platform with one foot and landing on two feet. If your children can handle stairs, they have probably already jumped down the stairs on their own. You might test them on a step or platform before going on. If they aren't successful, keep working on the Walking Up and Down Stairs activities for awhile.
- At the next stage of the vertical jump, the children push upward and slightly forward with their arms out for balance. They often stiffen their legs, which causes them to topple over when they land.
- As vertical jumping skills develop, the children start from a crouch with feet parallel and knees bent. They raise their arms above their heads and pull them down as they push off.

Gross Motor Movement 19 - Jumping & Landing

Primary Activity

- Demonstrate and describe the vertical jump. Then have the children do it with you. You will see a wide range of abilities. Practice with them until they can jump fairly well and then let them practice jumping in place.
- Encourage the children to see how high they can jump and how many times they can jump in place without stopping.

Levels Of Experience

- Let the children jump continuously.
- Try to do "light jumps" by pretending to be a little mouse jumping.

- Do "heavy jumps" by pretending to be an elephant jumping.
- Vary the speed of jumping.
- Tape off square areas on the floor. The children have to stay within the area as they jump.

- Have the children form a circle and you stand in the center. Call out the name of a child and say "(Sara), jump up" "(Sara), ¡salta hacia arriba!" as you slide a beanbag across the floor. The child must jump up and let the beanbag slide under his/her feet. If the child's feet touch the beanbag, he/she goes to the center and slides the beanbag.

Horizontal
A lo largo

Primary Skills & Concepts

Spatial and directional awareness, posture, awareness of body parts, movement of body parts, balance, flexibility, pushing, pulling

Materials

None

KEEP IN MIND

- The horizontal jump involves moving forward rather than up. The body leans forward and the arms swing in the direction of the jump, carrying it forward. Beginners have difficulty remembering to bend the legs after taking off.

Primary Activity

- Demonstrate and describe horizontal jumping. Stand in a crouch—the lower the crouch, the greater the force against the floor. Swing your arms back and then forward and up as you push off with your feet. Land with your legs bent, pulling your arms down.
- Let the children practice many times. Then let the children jump randomly around the area.

Levels Of Experience

- Place a hoop or rope on the floor and let the children jump in and out.
- Let the children jump over a rope placed at a variety of levels.

- Draw or tape two parallel lines about ten feet apart on the floor. Have the children line up outside one line. You stand outside the other line. Then name a color or an article of clothing. All children wearing that color or article of clothing jump as fast as they can to your line. The first child across gets to be the next leader.

- Draw or tape parallel lines about ten feet apart on the floor. Divide the group into three teams. Have the teams line up outside one line. Outside the other line put three piles of beanbags. On a signal the first child from each team jumps to the far line, grabs a beanbag, and jumps back to the starting line. The first team to get all of its beanbags home wins.

Kicking
Patear

Primary Skills & Concepts

Spatial and directional awareness, posture, awareness of body parts, movement of body parts, balance, flexibility, pushing, pulling, swinging

Materials

8" to 10" rubber balls or soccer balls

KICKING

Primary Activity

- Demonstrate and describe each level as you work with the child. At the most basic level, have the child stand near the ball, bend the knee of the dominant leg, push the ball with the foot, and return to the standing posture.
- After the child is able to do this fairly easily, have the child practice with the other leg.
- At the next level, the child stands near the ball with the legs bent, pulls the dominant leg backward, straightens it as the leg moves forward to strike the ball with the foot. The leg continues to move forward as a follow-through movement.
- Now the child will begin using the arms and legs in opposition as he/she moves the kicking leg forward. The child might also incorporate one or two steps toward the ball before kicking it.

LEVELS OF EXPERIENCE

- Vary the height to which the ball goes. The lower on the ball the foot kicks, the higher the ball goes.
- Kick with the toe.

- Kick with the inside of the foot.
- Kick toward a goal.

- Kick over an object.
- Kick the ball through an obstacle course.
- Kick the ball to a partner.

Hopping
Saltar en un pie

Primary Skills & Concepts

Spatial and directional awareness, posture, awareness of body parts, movement of body parts, balance, flexibility

Materials

None

KEEP IN MIND

- Hopping is difficult for most four-year-olds but they love to try. Technically, the child should push off from the floor with one foot and return to the floor on the same foot, landing on the toes and rolling to the ball of the foot. The inactive leg is bent and never touches the floor.
- About the most you can expect from a four-year-old is an unsteady gait. Often the child doesn't have enough strength or coordination to maintain balance on one leg while moving forward, so he/she will drop or drag the second foot or topple over. Children have to go through this stage, however, so you might as well let them start now.

Gross Motor Movement 22 - Hopping

Primary Activity

- Let the child hop randomly. At this level children probably won't have enough control to hop in a straight line or in a circle.

Levels Of Experience

- Hopping to music might help. As the children improve, increase the speed of the music.
- Encourage the children to practice starting and stopping by stopping the music periodically.

- Add hopping to your Follow the Leader and Simon Says games.

- Let those few children who are good hoppers try hopping in a circle and over ropes. Some might want to try hopping through a short obstacle course.

Bouncing
Rebotar

Primary Skills & Concepts

Spatial and directional awareness, posture, awareness of body parts, movement of body parts, balance, flexibility, pushing

Materials

8" to 10" rubber balls

KEEP IN MIND

- Always demonstrate and describe the mature action. A ball's bounce is controlled by the fingers and the wrists. The angle at which it is pushed determines the angle at which it rebounds. Therefore, to make the ball rebound straight upward, it must be pushed straight downward.
- Young children learn to bounce and trap a ball with two hands when they are about three years old. You will have many four-year-olds who need to work on this skill.

Ball Handling

Primary Activity

- Have the child stand with his/her feet about shoulder width apart, hold the ball with both hands at waist height, push the ball straight down, and trap the ball against the body when it rebounds. You'll notice that many children don't wait for the ball to rebound; they stoop to grab it. Until the child can consistently push and trap the ball with two hands, don't rush him/her to the next step.
- At the next level, the child holds the ball with one hand underneath and the other hand on top, pushes with one hand while releasing with the other. The child receives the ball with the hands and does not trap it.
- The child soon learns that he/she has better control of the ball when he/she spreads the pushing fingers and pushes with the fingers from the wrist. He/she will soon be able to use one hand consistently and to continuously push the ball back down and receive it with his/her fingertips.

Levels Of Experience

- Once the children pick up the bouncing pattern at any level, play music with a regular beat while they bounce. This will help them concentrate on the rhythm so they can bounce continuously.
- Let the children bounce to a pattern as you say it; for example, bounce, bounce, stop or bounce, stop, bounce, stop.
- Play Follow the Leader or Simon Says with bouncing balls.
- Let the children use smaller and larger rubber balls.
- Let the children experiment with walking or turning as they bounce.

Catching
Atrapar

Primary Skills & Concepts

Spatial and directional awareness, posture, awareness of body parts, movement of body parts, balance, flexibility, pushing, pulling

Materials

Beanbags or 8" to 10" rubber balls

Primary Activity

- Always demonstrate and describe the mature action. To catch a ball (beanbag), the child must stand behind or beneath the ball with palms toward the ball. When the ball is coming in high, the fingers curve up to trap it. When it is coming in low, the fingers bend down to scoop it. Catching and throwing are like the chicken and the egg—who knows which comes first. You will need to work individually with the children or pair them with those who already know the overhand throw.
- At the basic level, the child extends his/her arms and traps the ball against the chest with arms and hands.
- At the next level, the child extends his/her arms and catches the ball with the hands away from the body.
- Finally, the child moves toward the ball, catches it with the hands away from the body, and draws the ball in to the body on follow-through.

LEVELS OF EXPERIENCE

- Increase the distance between the tosser and the catcher.
- Increase the speed of the toss.

- Vary the levels of the toss.

- Have the children stand in a circle. You stand in the middle. Call out a child's name and toss him/her the ball. If the child catches the ball, he/she gets to name the next person to catch.

Overhand Throwing
Lanzamiento por lo alto

Primary Skills & Concepts

Spatial and directional awareness, posture, awareness of body parts, movement of body parts, balance, flexibility, pushing

Materials

Beanbags or 8" to 10" rubber balls

Primary Activity

- Always demonstrate and describe the mature action. The child's first attempt at throwing is usually a two-handed toss, probably overhand (the hands are over the ball) because it is an extension of dropping.
- At the basic level, the child starts the throw with the hand slightly behind the head and moves it over the shoulder and either straight down or diagonally across the front of the body.
- Later the child learns to step forward with the foot on the same side of the body as the throwing arm and releases the ball forward rather then downward or diagonally.
- The mature thrower steps forward on the opposing foot, twists slightly toward the throwing arm, releases the ball forward, and follows through with the throwing arm.

LEVELS OF EXPERIENCE

- Throw balls or beanbags at a large target such as a wall. As the child develops throwing skills, decrease the size of the target.

- Throw balls through hoops.
- Vary the distance from the target.
- Vary the speed of the throw.
- Throw to a partner.

- Throw balls, beanbags, or crumpled paper into a wastebasket.
- Vary the size of the balls or beanbags.
- Throw over a barrier such as a box or fence.

Underhand Throwing
Lanzamiento por lo bajo

Primary Skills & Concepts

Spatial and directional awareness, posture, awareness of body parts, movement of body parts, balance, flexibility, pushing

Materials

Beanbags or 8" to 10" rubber balls

Gross Motor Movement 26- Ball Handling

Primary Activity

- Always demonstrate and describe the mature action. It is easier to move an object forward using an underhand throw than an overhand throw, and it is probably easier for most people to use an underhand throw.
- At the early level, the child stands with arms apart, swings the throwing arm down and forward, releases the ball, and does not follow through.
- Later the child learns to step forward with the foot on the same side as the throwing arm while releasing the ball and following through.
- The mature thrower stands with feet together facing the target. As the throwing arm moves straight down and back, the body rotates slightly toward the throwing arm. As the throwing arm swings forward, the opposing leg moves forward to bear the body's weight. The ball is released when the hand reaches about the waist.

Levels Of Experience

- Throw balls or beanbags at a large target such as a wall. As the child develops throwing skills, decrease the size of the target.
- Throw balls through hoops.
- Vary the distance from the target.

- Vary the speed of the throw.
- Throw to a partner.

- Throw balls, beanbags, or crumpled paper into a wastebasket.
- Vary the size of the balls or beanbags.
- Throw over a barrier such as a box or fence.

Pounding
Dar golpes

Primary Skills & Concepts

Spatial and directional awareness, movement of body parts, eye-hand coordination

Materials

Sturdy pillow

KEEP IN MIND

- Fine motor skills are developed gradually with repeated practice, and one of the wonderful things about fine motor development is that most of it can be done through play and ordinary daily activities.
- Don't expect perfection; learning to control small muscles takes time.
- You will rarely encounter a four-year-old who can't pound with his/her fist. It is, however, an important part of many activities; it's a lot of fun; and it's a good way to vent anger and frustration. So you might want to give it a try even at the lowest levels.
- Babies probably discover pounding accidentally as they're swinging their arms around, and they begin with an open hand (a slap) and arms outstretched. Often you will notice babies pounding with both hands at once.
- Children should practice these motor skills hundreds of times. So use these activity suggestions as models for other activities.
- Always demonstrate and describe your movements so the child will know what is expected and can concentrate on improving.

Fine Motor Movement 1 - Pounding

Primary Activity

- You might want to start by having the child pound a sturdy pillow. Have the child hold his/her arm close to the body, raise the lower arm at the elbow, form a fist, and then drop the lower arm until the fist hits the pillow. After the child has done this several times, he/she will probably begin adding force to the drop; if not, encourage the child to "push hard" "¡Empuja fuerte!" with his/her arm. The stronger the force behind the push, the harder the fist will hit the pillow.

Levels Of Experience

- Let the child pound rhythmically as you count.
- Have the child pound with the non-dominant fist.

- Have the child alternate pounding with the dominant and non-dominant fists.
- Let the child pound on a drum.
- Have the child pound a ball of clay until it is flat.
- Have the child pound rhythmically to music.

- Pounding with a hammer or mallet is more difficult, especially if the child is trying to hit a specific object. Have the child practice pounding a large target, such as a ball of clay, before pounding a smaller target, such as pegs. Remind the child that he/she should hold the hammer or mallet near the butt of the handle, not near the head.

Picking Up & Releasing
Atrapar y soltar

Primary Skills & Concepts

Spatial and directional awareness, movement of body parts, eye-hand coordination

Materials

Block or ball that fits comfortably in the child's hand

Keep in Mind

- Grasping is a natural reflex. If you put something in a child's hand, the child closes his/her fingers around the object. Later the child notices an object, reaches for it, and touches it. When grasping is purposeful, it becomes a skill.
- You've witnessed, often with frustration, a child learning to release. Dropping a bottle from the highchair a hundred times a day is not orneriness—it's a necessary part of learning to control the release.

Fine Motor Movement 2 - Picking up & Releasing

Primary Activity

- After touching an object, the child grasps the object with his/her hand, holds it, and lifts it by raising the lower arm from the elbow. Sometimes you might have to help a child close his/her hand around the object and continue holding as you help the child lift the object. If a child has a great deal of difficulty, provide many opportunities for opening and closing the hands before going on with picking up and releasing. Finger plays are fun for developing this skill.
- After a child has picked up an object, have him/her open his/her hand. The object will drop out.
- When a child has mastered the drop release, have him/her pick up the object, lower the arm until the object touches a surface, and then open his/her hand.

Levels Of Experience

- When the child can pick up and release with the entire hand, have him/her try it using just the fingertips and then the tips of the index finger and thumb.
- Vary the sizes of the objects. Don't use small, flat objects such as coins, stickers, or stamps until the child has developed a great deal of control with larger objects.
- Building with blocks is a great way to develop these skills.
- Have the child pick up objects and put them into a container. Increase the difficulty by decreasing the size of the object and the size of the container.
- Hold relay races that involve picking up objects and putting them into a container such as a large box or basket.
- Have the child practice picking up and releasing cups containing dry objects such as beans, macaroni, or cotton balls. When the child can manipulate containers of dry objects, use liquids.
- Remember to use your sand and water tables.

Squeezing
Apretar

Primary Skills & Concepts

Spatial and directional awareness, movement of body parts, strength

Materials

A soft foam or rubber ball that fits comfortably in the child's hand

Keep in Mind

- Squeezing is an extension of grasping and requires more hand strength. In fact, squeezing is an excellent exercise for building hand strength.

Fine Motor Movement 3 - SQUEEZING

Primary Activity

- The child grasps the ball with his/her entire hand and closes the fingers tightly around the ball. At first, the child will be able to squeeze for only a few seconds before releasing. (Unless, of course, the child is holding on to something he/she wants to keep.) Encourage the child to squeeze until you count to 5, 10, 20, and then 30 seconds.

LEVELS OF EXPERIENCE

- Vary the size and hardness of the ball.
- Have the child practice squeezing with two hands.
- Let the child practice crumpling scrap paper before putting it into the recycling bin.

- Let the child practice squeezing empty plastic soda bottles. Later add water to the bottle to make squeezing more difficult.
- Shaking hands develops squeezing skill.
- Put sponges and dishrags in the water table for the children to squeeze.
- Let the children squeeze clay.

- Encourage the child to squeeze with his/her fingertips.
- On a warm day, take the children outside and let them use squeeze bottles or squirt bottles to squirt water at a target.
- Just for fun, let the children practice squeezing foam balls between their elbows or knees and with their feet.

Shaping
Dar forma

Primary Skills & Concepts

Spatial and directional awareness, movement of body parts, strength, eye-hand coordination, pounding, squeezing, pushing, pulling

Materials

Water-based clay

KEEP IN MIND

- Shaping clay or sand requires the combination of many fine motor skills. At this point, your concern is with the child's development of those skills, not with his/her ability to produce a recognizable image.
- Water-based clay is more pliable than oil-based clay; therefore, it is easier for young children to manipulate.

Primary Activity

- Give the child a large piece of clay and let him/her explore freely. Then encourage the child to try pounding, squeezing, pushing, pulling, and rolling the clay. Don't expect the child to be able to do all of these things without guidance. Demonstrate informally by talking about what you're doing. In time, the child will learn to shape several pieces of clay and put them together to form a larger image.

LEVELS OF EXPERIENCE

- Let the children use clay rather than crayons or paints to illustrate a character or scene from a story.

- Encourage the children to use mud or damp sand to shape and build objects.
- Make bread with the children and let them knead and shape the loaves.

- Add a tool such as a sturdy spoon to the shaping activities.

Fastening
Abrochar y desabrochar

Primary Skills & Concepts

Spatial and directional awareness, movement of body parts, eye-hand coordination, pushing, pulling

Materials

Strips of cloth with large snaps, clothing with snaps, strips of cloth with large buttons and buttonholes, clothing with buttons, zipper with bottom-end stop tacked to a board, clothing with zippers

KEEP IN MIND

- Snapping is a simple procedure that involves pushing, pulling, and eye-hand coordination. The most difficult part is positioning the stud and the socket, the two parts of a snap.
- Zipping a zipper with a bottom-end stop is relatively easy, especially if the zipper is attached to a board.
- Buttoning is the most difficult—it requires a great deal of dexterity. Use large buttons and large buttonholes.

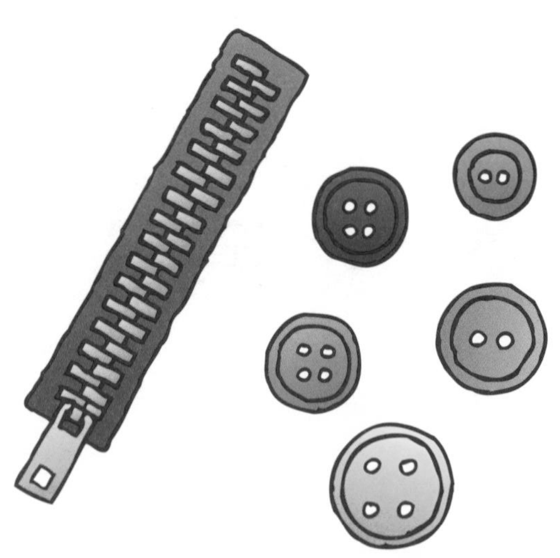

Primary Activity

- Show the two parts of a snap and point out that the post must snap into the socket. Demonstrate snapping by pushing the post into the socket with the thumb and index finger of one hand. Pull the pieces apart to demonstrate unsnapping. Let the child practice several times. Initially, the child might use the index fingers or thumbs on opposing hands.
- Let the child practice snapping and unsnapping the clothing you provided.
- Begin by demonstrating zipping and unzipping on the zipper board. Then let the child practice several times.
- When a zipper is loose or in a piece of clothing, zipping is more difficult. The secret to smooth zipping is to hold the bottom of the zipper firmly with one hand, pull down with that hand, and pull up the pull tab with the other hand. This will require a great deal of practice.
- Hold the button in the non-dominant hand and hold the fabric near the buttonhole with the dominant hand. Place the buttonhole over the button. Tilt the button upward and push it through the buttonhole. To unbutton, hold the button in the nondominant hand and the fabric near the buttonhole in the dominant hand. Tilt the button downward and slip it through the buttonhole. Demonstrate and describe the actions several times. Let the child practice several times as you repeat the directions.

LEVELS OF EXPERIENCE

- Put zipping, snapping, and buttoning boards in a learning center so children can practice.
- Put dolls and doll clothes in the home center so the children can practice dressing and undressing the dolls.
- Allow plenty of time for the children to practice fastening their own clothes. It will save you time and aggravation in the long run.

Fitting
Encajar

Primary Skills & Concepts

Spatial and directional awareness, movement of body parts, eye-hand coordination, pushing, pulling

Materials

Pegs and pegboards, nuts and bolts, locks and keys, puzzles, and toys such as Legos, Lincoln Logs, and Tinker Toys

Fine Motor Movement 6 - Fitting

Primary Activity

- Show the child a bolt with a nut on it. Demonstrate and describe removing the nut by twisting it counterclockwise with your index finger and thumb as you hold the bolt still with the other hand. Give the child a bolt with a nut and let him/her practice. Then demonstrate putting the nut on the bolt by twisting the nut clockwise. Let the child practice. Work with the child until he/she understands the process. Then allow plenty of center time for the child to practice.
- Follow similar procedures for each of the other manipulatives. Introduce no more than one manipulative a day. Make sure the child understands how to use the manipulative and then allow plenty of time for practice.

Levels Of Experience

- Do not hurry the child from one experience to the next. Allow him/her to work at the activity until he/she feels ready to move on.
- Vary the activity by increasing and decreasing the size of the manipulatives.

- Make bolt and nut boards. Drill holes of various sizes. Pound a bolt into each hole. Attach a nut to each bolt. Put the board in a learning center so the children can practice matching nuts and bolts and putting the nuts on and taking them off.

- Mount cup hooks to a board. Give the child several objects to hang on the hooks: keys, washers, rubber bands, and rubber jar rings.
- Put a variety of plastic bottles and lids into a cardboard box. Let the children match lids and bottles and practice putting the lids on and taking them off.

Spreading
Esparcir

Primary Skills & Concepts

Spatial and directional awareness, movement of body parts, eye-hand coordination

Materials

Smocks, fingerpainting supplies or colored water, tongue depressors, pudding or thin frosting, cookies or crackers

KEEP IN MIND

- Children begin spreading when they're very young; however, we call it smearing when it applies to cereal and pureed peas. Most four-year-olds will have no difficulty spreading with their hands.
- One good place to begin is with fingerpaints. Generally, children enjoy the way fingerpaints feel and delight in experimenting. There are some children, however, who find fingerpainting too messy because they don't enjoy getting their hands dirty. These children might find that they enjoy fingerpainting if they can wear disposable plastic gloves, or they might not mind fingerpainting with colored water.
- Spreading with a tool is a little more difficult. We suggest that you begin with a soft substance such as pudding and tongue depressors because they provide a wide surface.

Fine Motor Movement 7 - Spreading

Primary Activity

- Discuss and demonstrate fingerpainting. Show the children how to spread the paint, make designs, and erase them. Allow plenty of time for the children to experiment. Many will discover that they can use any number of fingers and the heel, palm, and fist to create interesting designs and patterns.
- Demonstrate and describe the procedure. Use the tongue depressor to scoop up a small amount of pudding. Place the pudding on a sturdy cracker or cookie. Spread the pudding with the tongue depressor. The children will need to practice many times, so you might want to let three or four children prepare the snacks each day. This way they each have the opportunity to spread five or six times. The children will tire of cookies with pudding or frosting so you might alternate snacks and use graham crackers and applesauce, soft jelly, soft margarine, cream cheese, and soft cheese spreads. Four-year-olds will have difficulty with rice cakes and peanut butter.

Levels Of Experience

- Let the children spread with plastic knives.
- Plan a picnic and let the children help prepare sandwiches. Use firm bread or toast to provide a firm surface for spreading.

- Painting with a brush provides practice in spreading.
- Let the children paint with shaving cream or whipped topping.
- Let the children make and spread mud at the water table.

- As a real challenge, let the children spread vegetable oil on waxed paper.
- If you're really brave, let the children spread shaving cream with their feet.

Pouring
Verter

Primary Skills & Concepts

Spatial and directional awareness, movement of body parts, eye-hand coordination

Materials

Small pitchers, sand or other pourable solids, cups, plastic glasses, plastic bowls, trays

KEEP IN MIND

- Let children begin pouring with dry solids, such as sand, aquarium gravel, or buttons. You might use beans, rice, and macaroni if you use these activites in conjunction with cooking so that you don't waste food.

Fine Motor Movement 8 - POURING

Primary Activity

- Set your containers on a tray to catch any overflow. Fill a small pitcher with sand and show the child how to pour the sand into a bowl. Emphasize that you are holding the pitcher with one hand and the bowl with the other. Pour slowly so the sand doesn't bounce out of the bowl. Let the child practice several times.
- Then demonstrate and let the child practice pouring sand into a variety of containers. When the child is able to pour with little difficulty, have him/her fill the container halfway and then to the top without spilling.

LEVELS OF EXPERIENCE

- Let the child pour other solids such as gravel, salt, and buttons.
- At the water table, let the child practice pouring liquids. You might want to begin with colored water so the child can see it easily.

- Let the children practice pouring fine solids and liquids through a funnel. You can make a funnel by cutting off the pouring end of a large plastic soft drink bottle about 4" from the opening.
- Let the children pour juice or milk at snack time.

- Add liquid soap to water and provide a variety of containers for the children to use at the water table.
- When cooking with the children, put as many ingredients as possible into containers so the children can pour them into the mixing bowl.

Folding
Doblar

Primary Skills & Concepts

Spatial and directional awareness, movement of body parts, eye-hand coordination

Materials

Magazine, socks, washcloths, paper napkins, construction paper

KEEP IN MIND

- Most children fold many things before they learn to fold paper. Precision folding is not as important for four-year-olds as understanding the concept.

Fine Motor Movement 9 - Folding

Primary Activity

- You might begin by showing an open magazine. As you close the magazine say "I am closing the magazine. I am folding the magazine. The outsides of the magazine are folded together. Now I can't see the inside."
  "Voy a cerrar la revista. La doblo. La tapa y la contratapa de la revista quedan unidas. No se pueden ver las páginas de la revista."
- Then show a sock. As you fold the sock say
  "I am folding the sock. See how the top of the sock touches the toe of the sock. Now I am going to press the fold with my hand to make the sock lie flat. Why might I want to fold socks?"
  "Voy a doblar las medias. Miren como la parte de arriba se une a la parte de abajo. Voy a aplanar la media con la mano. ¿Para qué necesito doblar las medias?"

  Let the child practice folding and unfolding socks. Encourage the child to describe what he/she is doing. Then let the child practice folding washcloths and paper napkins.
- After the child can fold items such as those mentioned above, let him/her work on folding paper. Color two opposing edges of a sheet of paper. Demonstrate and describe as you fold the paper by putting the two colored edges together and pressing the fold to flatten it. Give the child a similar sheet of paper and let him/her practice folding and creasing.
- Draw a dotted line across the middle of a sheet of paper. Demonstrate and describe folding and creasing the paper on the dotted line. As you fold, keep the dotted line on top so the child can see it.

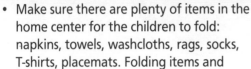

Levels Of Experience

- Make sure there are plenty of items in the home center for the children to fold: napkins, towels, washcloths, rags, socks, T-shirts, placemats. Folding items and putting them away is a natural part of cleanup.

- Let children fold napkins for snack time.
- Show the children how to fold paper into quarters.

- Fan folds are a little difficult for most four-year-olds, however, many children will be intrigued by the challenge and the results.
- Show the children how to fold the corners of a square sheet of paper to make a kite.
- Challenge the children to see how many times they can fold a sheet of paper. Who can make the smallest piece of paper?

Spooning
Usar una cuchara

Primary Skills & Concepts

Spatial and directional awareness, movement of body parts, eye-hand coordination

Materials

Soup spoons, sand or other spoonable solids, cups, plastic glasses, plastic bowls, trays

Spooning

Primary Activity

- Set your containers on a tray to catch any overflow. Fill a small bowl with sand and show the child how to spoon the sand into another bowl. Emphasize that you are holding the spoon with one hand and the bowl with the other. Work slowly so the sand doesn't spill. Let the child practice several times.
- Then demonstrate and let the child practice spooning sand into a variety of containers. When the child is able to spoon with little difficulty, have him/her fill the container halfway and then to the top without spilling.

Levels Of Experience

- Let the child spoon other solids such as gravel, salt, and small buttons.
- At the water table, let the child practice spooning liquids. You might want to begin with colored water so the child can see the water easily.
- Let the children practice spooning fine solids and liquids through a funnel. You can make a funnel by cutting off the pouring end of a large plastic soft drink bottle about 4" from the opening.

- Let the children spoon things like apple-sauce, raisins, and dry cereal at snack time.
- Provide a variety of containers for the children to use at the water table.
- When cooking with the children, let the children spoon ingredients into the mixing bowl.

- Hold relay races. Divide the children into teams. Give each team an empty bowl, a spoon, and a bowl full of buttons. Each team member in turn will move one spoonful of buttons from the first bowl into the second bowl. If buttons spill, the child must stop and pick them up. The first team to get all of the buttons out of the first bowl and into the second bowl wins.
- Use liquids in a spoon relay.

Tearing
Rasgar

Primary Skills & Concepts

Spatial and directional awareness, movement of body parts, eye-hand coordination

Materials

Newspaper or construction paper, cardboard box for scraps

Fine Motor Movement 11 - Tearing

Primary Activity

- Demonstrate and describe tearing. Hold a sheet of paper in the non-dominant hand near the place where you are going to tear. It's very difficult to control tearing when you are holding the paper far from where you plan to tear. With the other hand pull the paper forward or push it backward to tear. You are using the thumb and fingers on your non-dominant hand for leverage as you tear.
- Let the child practice making several tears. Have him/her put the torn paper into a box to use later for art projects or to line an animal's cage. At this stage, tearing will be random. Don't expect anything close to precision tearing until the child has done a great deal of random tearing.
- When the child has mastered random tearing, draw a line across the middle of a sheet of paper. Have the child fold and crease the paper on the line. Demonstrate tearing on the line. Most children will not be able to tear the paper in one movement; most of them will begin by tearing a little, moving their hands, and tearing again. To make a long tear, start the tear as usual, then move both hands to opposing sides of the paper. Pull one part of the paper forward as you push the other part backward.

Levels Of Experience

- Let the children tear different weights and textures of papers.
- Let the children tear pictures from old magazines for language, math, and science projects.
- Let the children tear lettuce for a salad.

- When the children are eating soft cookies or bread as a snack, encourage them to tear off small pieces and to eat one piece at a time.
- Each week assign a child the job of tearing paper to put in the bottom of an animal's cage.

- Draw large, simple shapes on construction paper so the children can tear out shapes. Use the shapes in art projects or for sorting in the science or math center.
- Make a torn-paper mural. The children can tear clouds, trees, and grass. Those who are proficient paper tearers can tear other objects. Add details with paints, crayons, or markers.

Cutting
Cortar

Primary Skills & Concepts

Spatial and directional awareness, movement of body parts, eye-hand coordination

Materials

Left-handed and right-handed scissors, newspaper or construction paper, cardboard box for scraps

Fine Motor Movement 12 - Cutting

Primary Activity

- Before having a child actually cut with scissors, let him/her practice opening and closing the scissors. Give the child the appropriate pair of scissors. Demonstrate and describe holding scissors. The thumb goes in the small hole. The index finger rests against the top and on the outside of the large hole. The two or three remaining fingers go in the large hole. To open the scissors, lift the thumb; to close the scissors, lower the thumb.
- Demonstrate and describe cutting. Hold a sheet of paper in the non-dominant hand. Hold the scissors in the dominant hand. Open the scissors and slip the sheet of paper between the blades. Close the scissors. The wider the blades are apart, the longer the cut.
- Work with the child to cut pieces from a sheet of paper. If necessary, hold your hands over the child's hands until he/she gets the feel and rhythm of cutting. Then let the child have many opportunities for random cutting before proceeding.
- When the child has mastered random cutting, draw a line across the middle of a sheet of paper. Have the child fold and crease the paper on the line. Then show the child how to cut on the line. Most children will not be able to cut the paper in one movement; they will cut a little, reposition their paper and scissors and cut some more.

Levels Of Experience

- Have the children cut paper for art projects.
- Challenge the children to cut tiny bits of paper.
- Give the children different weights and textures of papers to cut.

- Let the children cut pictures from old magazines for language, math, and science projects.
- Draw straight lines and simple curves for the children to cut along.

- Let the children use scissors instead of cookie cutters to cut out sugar cookies.
- Let the children cut a variety of materials such as yarn, ribbon, and sponges. They can use these pieces in art projects.

Tracing
Trazar

Primary Skills & Concepts

Spatial and directional awareness, movement of body parts, eye-hand coordination

Materials

Unlined paper, pencils/crayons, simple geometric templates and stencils

Fine Motor Movement 13 - TRACING

Primary Activity

- Demonstrate and describe as you trace around your hand. Place a sheet of paper on the table. Put your non-dominant hand on the paper and spread your fingers. Trace your hand with a crayon or pencil. Go slowly and trace as closely as you can. Then let the child trace his/her own hand. If necessary, help the child by guiding the hand with which he/she is tracing. You might want to have the child trace his/her foot.
- Demonstrate and describe tracing with a template. A template is easier than a stencil because you trace inside a boundary. By pressing your pencil or crayon against the border of the template as you trace, you have more control. Remind the child to hold the template and the paper still with one hand while tracing with the other. Young children will probably turn the paper and template rather than move the pencil around the template. When the child is able to trace well this way, encourage him/her to hold the paper still and move the pencil.
- Demonstrate and describe tracing with a stencil. Remind the child to hold the stencil and the paper still with one hand while tracing with the other. Again, the child is likely to move the paper and stencil rather than the pencil.

LEVELS OF EXPERIENCE

- Increase the complexity of the templates and stencils the child traces.
- Let the child trace around other objects such as blocks, saucers, and kitchen utensils.

- Provide a variety of textures for the child to trace on.
- Let the child trace shapes onto fabrics.
- Make simple dot-to-dot drawings for the child to trace. Begin with the dots about 1/2" apart. As the child becomes proficient, increase the distance between the dots.

- At this age, many children will be able to trace shapes and block letters. Use a wide, dark marker and draw a shape or letter on a sheet of paper. Let the child trace the shape.
- Draw simple mazes for the children to trace.

Copying
Copiar

Primary Skills & Concepts

Spatial and directional awareness, movement of body parts, eye-hand coordination

Materials

Unlined paper, pencils/crayons

KEEP IN MIND

- You might have a few four-year-olds who are ready for copying; however, this is difficult so don't expect it. Copying means making a reproduction while looking at a shape or object that is adjacent or at a distance, as opposed to tracing in which you are working directly on the shape or object.

Primary Activity

- Demonstrate and describe as you copy a short straight line. Some people find it easier to keep their eyes on the object while copying; others prefer to look at the object, or part of it, and then draw the object.
- After a child can copy a short straight line, move on to longer lines, simple curves, and simple combinations.

LEVELS OF EXPERIENCE

- Above are designs in ascending order of difficulty for the child to copy.
- Vary the difficulty of copying by increasing the distance between the child and the design or object he/she is copying.
- Vary the size of the writing instrument.